COLLECTOR'S ENCYCLOPEDIA OF

CHILDREN'S DISHES

AN ILLUSTRATED VALUE GUIDE

Margaret and Kenn Whitmyer

COLLECTOR BOOKS
P.O. Box 3009
Paducah, KY 42002-3009

Dedication

This book is dedicated to our sons, Quentin and Bryan, who persevered through this project.

The current values in this book should be used only as a guide. They are not intended to set prices, which vary from one section of the country to another. Auction prices as well as dealer prices vary greatly and are affected by condition as well as demand. Neither the Authors nor the Publisher assumes responsibility for any losses that might be incurred as a result of consulting this guide.

Searching For A Publisher?

We are always looking for knowledgeable people considered to be experts within their fields. If you feel that there is a real need for a book on your collectible subject and have a large comprehensive collection, contact Collector Books.

Additional copies of this book may be ordered from:

COLLECTOR BOOKS
P.O. Box 3009
Paducah, KY 42002-3009

or

Margaret and Kenn Whitmyer
P.O. Box 30806
Gahanna, OH 43230
@ $19.95 Add $2.00 for postage and handling.

Copyright: Margaret and Kenn Whitmyer, 1993
Values updated 1995

COLLECTOR'S ENCYCLOPEDIA OF

CHILDREN'S DISHES

AN ILLUSTRATED VALUE GUIDE

Contents

Acknowledgments

We would like to take this opportunity to express our appreciation to the many people who helped make this book possible. Enthusiastic collectors and dealers from all over the country shared their collections, welcomed us into their homes, and spent many hours discussing their collections.

We would especially like to acknowledge the fine work of Mary Lou Esterline. Her vast knowledge of pattern glass and china proved invaluable and saved us many hours of exhausting research. We deeply appreciate her time and effort.

We also greatly appreciate the hospitality extended to us by Parke and Joyce Bloyer, Jim and Nancy Maben, and George and Roni Sionakides. They invited us into their homes and spent many hours packing glass which enabled us to photograph their extensive collections. Also, they contributed historical information, ideas, and helped with pricing.

We also wish to thank the many antique dealers who contacted us with interesting items. Especially helpful were Bruce Knight of Knight's Antiques, Springfield, Ohio and Fred Altevogt of the Greater Columbus Antique Mall, Columbus, Ohio. They have helped to make this book more complete and their contributions are deeply appreciated.

We are also very grateful to the following people who either loaned us items to photograph or supplied us with valuable information:

Ann Barnes
Miles Bausch
Fred Bickenheuser
Bill Cass
Marietta Dalessandro
John and Rita Ebner
Betty Eichhorn
Don and Linda Fagley
Gene and Cathy Florence
Justine Geiser
Bill Heacock
William Horton
Joyce Johnson
Jack and Dorothy Jordan
Ann Kerr
Lorrie Kitchen and Dan Tucker
Scott and Mary Kuder
Nora Koch

Jim LaMeroeoux
Merle and Dee Long
Bill and Minerva Lesher
Douglas Lucas
Jim Massie
Fred McMorrow
Jimmy McRae
Ray and Nadine Pankow
Jo Ann Porter
Gerry Pugh
Merrill Rosander
Marilyn Ross
Judy Smith
Dick and Verylene Summers
Rick Teets
Bunnie Walker
Delmer and Mary Lou Youngen

Foreword

The purpose of this book is to give the collector a general idea of what is available, and at what prices children's dishes might be obtained. Included are sections on glass, china, metal, stoneware, and plastic. An attempt has been made to identify the manufacturer, when possible. We have also tried to identify reproductions and new issues.

Although as many sets as possible have been included in each area, there is no possible way any one book on children's dishes could be complete. New discoveries are being made every day, and we hope to be able to share some of them with you in the future.

Pricing

The prices in this book represent average retail prices for mint condition pieces. A price range has been included to allow for some regional differences in price. This book is intended to be only a guide and is not intended to set or establish prices.

Most sets have been priced both as sets and again with prices for each piece in the set. Since many sets are very difficult to complete, prices for the individual pieces may prove somewhat unrealistic if the pieces are removed from the confines of a set. For example, in many of the china sets, individual saucers, plates or even cups may have little value. Many collectors have become reluctant to buy odd pieces, therefore, the closer a set is to being complete, the greater the value of the individual components and the easier it is to sell.

The prices listed are prices we have seen collectors pay, and also, prices collectors have told us they would be willing to pay.

Reproductions and New Creations

Compared to the number of items available in children's dishes, reproductions have not been a widespread problem. All pieces that we know have been reproduced will be noted, and the new colors will be indicated in a footnote.

In recent years, various individuals have created miniature pieces and introduced them to the collectible market. These items, which are generally made of glass, are usually sold by reputable dealers who represent them as new to their loyal clientele. Therefore, these innovations have found their niche among collectors, and generally only pose a problem to novice collectors.

New china sets may also be found. These are generally from Japan, Taiwan, or some other Far East country. They are most easily identified as newer by their shape, size, and the quality of decoration.

Measurements

All measurements have been taken as follows to the nearest $1/16$":

Bowl – diameter
Butter – height to top of lid
Cakestand – height
Casserole – total length including handles
Creamer – height to highest point
Cup – height
Pitcher – height to highest point
Plate – diameter

Platter – length
Saucer – diameter
Spooner – height
Sugar, open – height
Sugar and lid – height with lid
Teapot and lid – height to top of lid
Tray – diameter
Waste bowl – height

PART 1: GLASS
Akro Agate Company

The Akro Agate Company was established in Akron, Ohio, in 1911. The first products of this new company were marbles and games. In 1914, the company moved to Clarksburg, West Virginia, to reap the benefits of cheaper natural gas. The company remained at this site until it closed its doors in 1951.

During the depths of the Great Depression when business was slow and competition from other marble producers was intense, Akro began to experiment with new products. Innovative colored glass doll dish sets were produced but never gained wide public acceptance until the forties when World War II created severe raw material shortages and curtailed the cheap foreign imports. However, the prosperity was short-lived. The Akro Agate Company was not able to survive the return of peacetime, which resulted in the resumption of cheap imports and the introduction of plastics.

Most children's pieces, except those which were made exclusively for J. Pressman, will bear the Akro Agate trademark – a crow flying through the letter "A." Generally most sets will be found in two sizes, which collectors have termed "large" and "small." Large-size sets will contain pieces which are slightly bigger than their counterparts in the small-size sets. Also, the large sets will usually contain cereal bowls and sugars with lids. Sugars in the small-size sets do not have lids and some small-size sets may contain a pitcher and tumblers.

Akro Agate children's sets were sold in many different size boxes. Some of the more common boxed sets include:

7-piece – open teapot or pitcher, 2 cups and saucers, 2 plates (Raised Daisy sets only)
7-piece – pitcher and 6 tumblers
8-piece – teapot and lid, 2 cups and saucers, 2 plates
10-piece – teapot and lid, 2 cups and saucers, creamer and open sugar, 2 plates (small-size sets)
12-piece – teapot and lid, 4 cups and saucers, creamer and open sugar (small-size sets)
13-piece – open teapot or pitcher, 4 cups and saucers, 4 plates (Raised Daisy sets only)
16-piece – teapot and lid, 4 cups and saucers, 4 plates, creamer and open sugar (small-size sets)
17-piece – teapot and lid, 4 cups and saucers, 4 plates, creamer, sugar and lid (large size sets)
19-piece – open teapot or pitcher, 4 cups and saucers, 4 plates, creamer, open sugar, 4 tumblers (Raised Daisy sets only)
21-piece – teapot and lid, 4 cups and saucers, 4 plates, creamer, sugar and lid, 4 cereal bowls
21-piece – teapot and lid, 4 cups and saucers, 4 plates, creamer and open sugar, pitcher, 4 tumblers
22-piece – teapot and lid, 6 cups and saucers, 6 plates, creamer and open sugar
28-piece – teapot and lid, 6 cups and saucers, 6 plates, creamer and open sugar, 6 tumblers

Innovative packaging was an Akro Agate specialty. Therefore, other boxed combinations are likely to be found. Notice several boxed combinations were sold without a sugar and creamer. This helps to explain why collectors are finding a shortage of some sugars and creamers.

J. Pressman Pastry Sets

The J. Pressman Company of New York marketed several child's pastry sets which incorporated glass pieces produced by the Akro Agate Company. Three of the sets are pictured here. It should be noted that complete boxed pastry sets are most desirable and individual pieces out of their original boxes retain very little value.

Pastry Set No. 7342

This set contains an open opaque green mixing bowl, a wooden rolling pin, several wooden utensils, a cutting board, two metal cookie cutters, and a recipe sheet.
Boxed Set $75.00-95.00

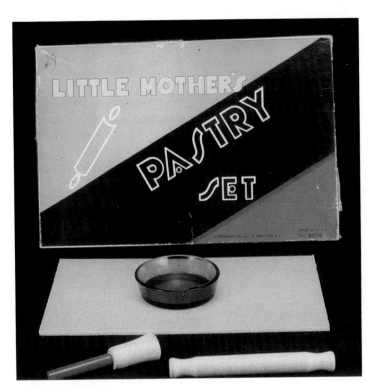

Pastry Set No. 2902

Retail price of this set in the 1930's was 29 cents. A cobalt Akro mixing bowl was included in this box.
Boxed Set $75.00-95.00

Little Mother's Pastry Set

This deluxe version of Pressman's Pastry Set has two opaque green Akro Agate bowls. There is an open mixing bowl and a covered bowl. Metal pieces include a cake tin for funnel cakes and two cookie cutters. A recipe sheet, cutting board, and wooden utensils complete the set.
Boxed Set $175.00-200.00

"Tea for Six"

The Akro Agate Company produced the glass pieces used in these tea sets for the J. Pressman Company. The cups and saucers used in this set may be found in a variety of colors and were also used in demitasse sets. Only opaque green cups and saucers have been found boxed with the children's sets. The cups and saucers have a crude appearance and attract very little collector interest outside of boxed sets.

Tea for Six	Opaque Green
Cup	$4.00-6.00
Saucer	$2.00-2.50
Boxed Set, 12 pieces	$40.00-60.00

The large-size child's pieces pictured in the right side of the photo were produced exclusively for the J. Pressman Company of New York. Most commonly sets included pieces with brightly baked-on colors over a crystal base, but sets have also been found in transparent green, transparent brown, transparent red, and clear blue. Occasional pieces of blue-tinted crystal are also found.

The rarer transparent colored sets are commanding high prices while many of the sets comprised of baked-on colors go begging for buyers. The most common baked-on color combinations are red cups, yellow saucers, green plates, a blue teapot and blue lid, blue creamer, blue sugar, and red cereal bowls.

The cobalt set on the left with the vertical ribs appears to be a J.P. type set but may not have been made by Akro Agate. This set has no teapot or sugar and creamer.

J.P.	Light Blue/ Crystal	Baked-on Colors	Trans Cobalt w/Ribs
Cereal, 3¹³⁄₁₆"		$9.00-11.00	
Creamer, 1½"	$27.50-32.50	$7.00-9.00	
Cup, 1½"	$18.00-20.00	$5.50-8.00	$6.00-8.00
Plate, 4¼"	$8.50-10.00	$4.00-5.00	$4.50-6.00
Saucer, 3¼"	$4.00-5.00	$1.25-1.50	$2.00-2.50
Sugar, 1½"	$27.00-32.00	$10.00-12.50	
Teapot and Lid, 2¾"	$40.00-50.00	$18.00-22.00	
Boxed Set, 17 pieces	$210.00-245.00	$80.00-110.00	
Boxed Set, 21 pieces		$120.00-150.00	

The two cups and saucers in the bottom of this photo are the only pieces of marbleized "J.P." we know about. A whole set in this blue-green color would be very unusual.

Many of the complete transparent green, brown, and red J.P. sets have been found in Little Orphan Annie boxes. In this case both the child's sets and the box could be considered rare, and an original box in good condition would add considerable value to an already expensive set.

Sugar lids have been found in the elusive transparent colors but are either non-existent or very rare in the more common baked-on sets.

J.P.	Transparent Green	Transparent Red/Brown
Creamer, 1½"	$40.00-45.00	$45.00-55.00
Cup, 1½"	$16.00-19.00	$22.00-25.00
Plate, 4¼"	$10.00-12.00	$13.00-15.00
Saucer, 3¼"	$4.50-6.00	$7.00-9.00
Sugar and Lid, 1½"	$45.00-50.00	$55.00-65.00
Teapot and Lid, 2¾"	$60.00-70.00	$75.00-95.00
Boxed Set, 17 pieces	$260.00-305.00	$340.00-400.00

Blue marble cup and saucer $100.00-125.00

Chiquita

"Chiquita" sets were made for the J. Pressman Company of New York. Although mold flaws, bubbles, and extreme color differences are characteristic of the pieces in these sets, many of the sets were marketed in attractive, brightly colored boxes. Perhaps the eye-catching boxes were designed to hide the crudeness of the glass within them. A few interesting combinations of boxed sets have been found. One is a 22-piece set in opaque green. This set includes a teapot and lid, a creamer and an open sugar, six cups and saucers, and six plates. Another set which has appeared in transparent cobalt lacks dinner plates. It consists of a teapot and lid, a creamer and an open sugar, and four cups and saucers.

The most commonly found color is opaque green. Other opaque colors such as lavender, light blue, turquoise, caramel, and yellow are difficult to collect. Transparent cobalt is the second most frequently found color. Sets with bake-on colors, such as the set in the right of the photo, are not easy to find. The four colors of this set are baked-on over a bluish-tinted crystal base. This may explain the existence of the few light transparent blue pieces such as the teapot bottom in the lower right corner of the photograph. Most of these pieces probably received the baked-on treatment. The boxed set on the left included a tablecloth and napkins which could be embroidered. They are shown in the top center of the photo.

Few collectors are interested in the drabbly colored opaque green sets and the price for these sets remains low. The higher prices for the cobalt sets are reflected by the desire of many people to own a reasonably priced cobalt child's set. Prices for the difficult to find opaque colors are creeping higher.

Chiquita	Green Opaque	Other Opaques	Transparent Cobalt*	Baked-on Colors
Creamer, 1½"	$4.00-5.00	$16.00-18.00	$14.00-16.00	$5.00-8.00
Cup, 1½"	$3.00-4.00	$12.00-14.00	$6.00-8.00	$5.00-6.00
Plate, 3¾"	$2.50-3.00		$5.00-7.00	$2.00-3.00
Saucer, 3⅛"	$1.50-2.00	$3.00-5.00	$3.00-3.50	$1.50-1.75
Sugar, no Lid, 1½"	$4.00-5.00	$16.00-18.00	$14.00-16.00	$5.00-8.00
Teapot and Lid, 3"	$12.00-14.00	$35.00-40.00	$25.00-30.00	$20.00-22.00
Boxed Set, 12 pieces		$127.00-150.00	$85.00-104.00	
Boxed Set, 16 pieces	$48.00-58.00		$108.00-137.00	$65.00-84.00
Boxed Set, 22 pieces	$62.00-78.00			

Tablecloth and 4 napkins, $25.00 set   *Crystal, 50% higher

Concentric Rib

"Concentric Rib" sets are only available in the small size. Cups, saucers, and plates in this set have a band with a series of narrowly spaced rings. Sets are completed with the use of a "Stacked Disc" covered teapot, sugar, and creamer. Colors of the pieces in many sets are opaque green and white. Other colors available include opaque pink and opaque blue with the teapots and sugars and creamers appearing in the full range of "Stacked Disc" colors.

Many times there is confusion in distinguishing between "Concentric Rib" and "Concentric Ring" sets. Pieces of "Concentric Rib" are of significantly poorer quality than those of "Concentric Ring." Also, "Concentric Rib" sets contain a "Stacked Disc" covered teapot, sugar and creamer, while the "Concentric Ring" sets have a "Stacked Disc and Interior Panel" covered teapot, sugar, and creamer.

Concentric Rib	Opaque Green/White	Other Opaque Colors
Creamer, 1¼"	$8.00-10.00	$14.00-16.00
Cup, 1¼"	$4.00-5.00	$6.00-8.00
Plate, 3¼"	$2.50-3.50	$6.00-7.00
Saucer, 2¾"	$1.50-2.00	$2.00-2.50
Sugar, no Lid, 1¼"	$8.00-10.00	$14.00-16.00
Teapot and Lid, 3⅜"	$10.00-12.00	$16.00-18.00
Boxed Set, 8 pieces	$26.00-33.00	$45.00-54.00
Boxed Set, 10 pieces	$42.00-53.00	$74.00-87.00

Concentric Ring, Large and Small

"Concentric Ring" cups, saucers, and plates are characterized by a series of closely spaced horizontal raised rings. The creamer, sugar, teapot, and lids are the same as "Stacked Disc and Interior Panel." Pieces have a superior quality and luster which is lacking in the similarly designed "Concentric Rib" pieces.

Solid opaque "Concentric Ring" large-size sets are attractively boxed in a multitude of bright colors. Opaque colored small-size sets with yellow or lavender cups are virtually non-existent and blue marbleized sets in either size are almost impossible to find.

In the photo on the next page, the boxed set and the lavender cup are large-size. The remainder of the pieces are small-size. The lavender cup in the foreground of the photo below is unusual. Its concentric rings continue all the way to the base of the cup instead of being confined to a narrow ring around the center. It also has interior panels which is unlike other cups of this style.

Large-Size Concentric Ring	Transparent Cobalt	Blue Marbleized	Solid Opaque Colors
Cereal, 3⅜"	$30.00-35.00	$40.00-45.00	$22.00-25.00
Creamer, 1⅜"	$30.00-35.00	$45.00-50.00	$14.00-16.00
*Cup, 1⅜"	$30.00-35.00	$35.00-40.00	$25.00-30.00
Plate, 4¼"	$18.00-20.00	$20.00-25.00	$6.00-7.00
Saucer, 3⅛"	$7.00-10.00	$12.00-15.00	$4.00-5.00
Sugar and Lid, 1⅞"	$45.00-55.00	$60.00-70.00	$20.00-27.00
Teapot and Lid, 3¾"	$65.00-70.00	$100.00-125.00	$40.00-45.00
Boxed Set, 21 pieces	$480.00-560.00	$623.00-745.00	$295.00-350.00

*Pumpkin, $50.00; yellow, $27.50; lavender, $27.50

Concentric Ring, Large and Small

Small-Size Concentric Ring	Transparent Cobalt	Blue Marbleized	Solid Opaque Colors
Creamer, 1¼"	$30.00-35.00	$35.00-40.00	$18.00-20.00
Cup, 1¼"	$27.00-30.00	$30.00-35.00	$8.00-10.00
Plate, 3¼"	$18.00-20.00	$20.00-22.00	$4.00-6.00
Saucer, 2¾"	$8.00-10.00	$10.00-12.00	$2.50-3.50
Sugar, 1¼"	$30.00-35.00	$35.00-40.00	$18.00-20.00
Teapot and Lid, 3⅜"	$45.00-50.00	$100.00-125.00	$30.00-37.00
Boxed Set, 16 pieces	$305.00-360.00	$410.00-480.00	$125.00-160.00

Interior Panel, Small

Pieces of Akro Agate's "Interior Panel" pattern have panels on the tops of plates and saucers, and inside of cups, sugars, creamers, teapots, lids, pitchers, and tumblers. The back sides of the plates and saucers and the exteriors of the other pieces are smooth. The pitcher and tumblers are frequently found in transparent green and amber, but only a few opaque tumblers have been seen. Notice the two different styles of pitchers and tumblers shown in transparent green. One style has vertical panels which continue to the top edge. In the other type there is a horizontal band around the top edge which lacks vertical panels. Some pieces of this pattern may also have stippled rings around the top edge. Collectors are calling these pieces "Stippled Interior Panel" (see "Stippled Band," small).

Commonly found boxed sets include the eight-piece, two-place setting with a teapot and lid, but lacking a sugar and creamer; and the 16-piece set with a four-place setting. Note that the marketing of the eight-piece sets without the sugar and creamer has resulted in a shortage of sugars and creamers for today's collectors.

Interior panel teapots, creamers, and sugars may be found with or without vertical darts on their exterior surface. This difference may cause collectors some problems when they are buying individual pieces to complete sets.

Small-size Interior Panel	Pink Luster	Azure Blue/ Yellow	Green Luster/ Transparent Green/Topaz
Creamer, 1¼"	$22.00-27.00	$32.00-35.00	$15.00-20.00
Cup, 1¼"	$10.00-12.00	$27.00-30.00	$8.00-10.00
Pitcher, 2⅞"			$12.00-14.00
Plate, 3¾"	$4.00-6.00	$8.00-10.00	$3.00-4.00
Saucer, 2⅜"	$3.00-4.00	$5.00-7.00	$3.00-3.50
Sugar, 1¼"	$22.00-27.00	$30.00-35.00	$15.00-20.00
Teapot and Lid, 3⅜"	$25.00-30.00	$45.00-55.00	$18.00-22.00
Tumbler, 2"	$50.00-55.00		*$6.00-8.50
Boxed Set, 8 pieces	$60.00-75.00	$115.00-133.00	$45.00-57.00
Boxed Set, 16 pieces	$148.00-178.00	$265.00-298.00	$103.00-132.00

Pumpkin cup $20.00; Opaque cobalt teapot/white lid $40.00-45.00;

Opaque cobalt sugar $25.00; Opaque cobalt creamer $25.00.

*Green luster $50.00-55.00

Interior Panel, Small

Small-size Interior Panel	Blue & White Marbleized	Red & White Marbleized	Green & White Marbleized
Creamer, 1¼"	$27.00-30.00	$32.00-35.00	$20.00-22.00
Cup, 1¼"	$22.00-24.00	$25.00-27.00	$10.00-12.00
Pitcher, 2⅞"			
Plate, 3¾"	$10.00-14.00	$10.00-12.00	$8.00-10.00
Saucer, 2⅜"	$7.00-10.00	$7.00-10.00	$5.00-6.00
Sugar, 1¼"	$27.00-30.00	$32.00-35.00	$20.00-22.00
Teapot and Lid, 3⅜"	$40.00-50.00	$40.00-50.00	$25.00-35.00
Tumbler, 2"			
Boxed Set, 8 pieces	$115.00-145.00	$125.00-148.00	$70.00-90.00
Boxed Set, 16 pieces	$253.00-290.00	$272.00-315.00	$157.00-190.00

Interior Panel, Large

"Interior Panel" pieces have vertical lines forming panels on the tops of plates and saucers, and inside of bowls, cups, sugars, creamers, teapots, and lids. "Interior Panel" differs from "Stacked Disc and Interior Panel" since all "Interior Panel" pieces are smooth on the undersides of plates and saucers, and on the exterior sides of other pieces. Large-size sets include cereal bowls and sugar lids. The sugar lid is the same as the small-size teapot lid.

There are two different shades of the topaz color – light yellow and a deep amber. When collectors are piecing a set together it is sometimes difficult to match up colors of the various pieces. Although the marbleized colors are the most highly prized among collectors, all colors of "Interior Panel" are very collectible. Opaque yellow teapots, sugars, creamers, and cups are scarce. Some transparent red pieces have been found. Not enough pieces have surfaced to establish realistic prices or to offer evidence that this color was ever produced commercially.

Large-size Interior Panel	Blue & White Marbleized	Red & White Marbleized	Green & White Marbleized
Cereal, 3⅜"	$30.00-35.00	$32.00-37.00	$22.00-25.00
Creamer, 1⅜"	$32.00-37.00	$40.00-45.00	$20.00-25.00
Cup, 1⅜"	$20.00-25.00	$30.00-32.00	$15.00-18.00
Plate, 4¼"	$14.00-16.00	$16.00-18.00	$15.00-18.00
Saucer, 3⅛"	$7.00-10.00	$8.00-10.00	$6.00-7.00
Sugar and Lid, 1⅞"	$40.00-50.00	$50.00-60.00	$30.00-35.00
Teapot and Lid, 3¾"	$65.00-75.00	$90.00-110.00	$45.00-55.00
Boxed Set, 21 pieces	$425.00-500.00	$525.00-600.00	$289.00-345.00

Large-size Interior Panel	Lemonade & Oxblood	Transparent Green	Transparent Topaz
Cereal, 3⅜"	$30.00-32.00	$13.00-15.00	$10.00-12.00
Creamer, 1⅜"	$35.00-40.00	$22.00-25.00	$20.00-22.00
Cup, 1⅜"	$20.00-25.00	$7.00-9.00	$7.00-9.00
Plate, 4¼"	$12.00-15.00	$5.00-6.00	$4.00-5.00
Saucer, 3⅛"	$8.00-10.00	$3.00-4.00	$2.00-3.50
Sugar and Lid, 1⅞"	$45.00-50.00	$27.00-32.00	$25.00-27.00
Teapot and Lid, 3¾"	$65.00-75.00	$35.00-40.00	$30.00-35.00
Boxed Set, 21 pieces	$425.00-495.00	$182.00-215.00	$165.00-200.00

Refer to the next page for prices of solid opaque colors.

Interior Panel, Large

Shown in the photograph above are the "Interior Panel" sets commonly referred to as the "luster sets." These pieces have a shinier appearance than most other Akro children's dishes. The green is lighter and more translucent than the green in the boxed set on the previous page.

Large-size Interior Panel	Pink & **Green Luster	Azure Blue Yellow Opaque
Cereal, 3⅜"	$20.00-25.00	$30.00-32.00
Creamer, 1⅜"	$25.00-27.00	$25.00-35.00
Cup, 1⅜"	$14.00-15.00	$25.00-35.00
Plate, 4¼"	$6.00-9.00	$7.00-10.00
Saucer, 3⅛"	$3.00-4.00	$5.00-7.00
Sugar and Lid, 1⅞"	$30.00-35.00	*$45.00-50.00
Teapot and Lid, 3¾"	$40.00-45.00	*$55.00-65.00
Boxed Set, 21 pieces	$265.00-320.00	$385.00-467.00

*Cobalt opaque with white lid 20% less

**Flat green 20% less

Miss America

Sets of "Miss America" are very difficult to find. Part of the difficulty in finding these pieces may be due to the unusual shape of the pieces and the lack of the identifying Akro trademark on many of them. The style is not characteristic of Akro and most of the pieces we have seen do not bear the Akro mark. The plates and saucers have a very thick outer rim. The rim on the plate is about ⅝" wide and the one on the saucer is about ⁵⁄₁₆" wide. The plates in the boxed set do not have any markings. The teapot, sugar, creamer, and cups have a backstamp which consists of a number and the initials "U.S.A." Both the teapot and the sugar have lids. Handles are open and square in shape. The cup, sugar, creamer, and teapot have a small foot. Colors available are forest green, white opaque, white opaque with decals, and orange marbleized.

Miss America	White	Orange & White Forest Green White with Decal
Creamer, 1¼"	$45.00-50.00	$55.00-65.00
Cup, 1⅝"	$35.00-40.00	$45.00-50.00
Plate, 4½"	$20.00-25.00	$40.00-45.00
Saucer, 3⅝"	$10.00-15.00	$12.00-15.00
Sugar and Lid, 2"	$55.00-65.00	$75.00-85.00
Teapot and Lid, 3¼"	$75.00-85.00	$125.00-140.00
Boxed Set, 17 pieces	$430.00-515.00	$560.00-650.00

Octagonal, Large

There are two styles of "Octagonal" large-size sets. The sets are distinguished by the type of handle of the cups, teapots, sugars, and creamers. These pieces may be found with either open or closed handles. The plates, saucers, cereal bowls, and lids to both sets are the same. Open handle "Octagonal" sets are sometimes referred to as "Octagonal-O." Both styles are found in a wide array of opaque colors, but the lemonade and oxblood color has only been found with closed handle pieces. Also the commonly found opaque green and white sets will usually have closed handles. The 21-piece boxed set includes cereal bowls while the 17-piece boxed set does not.

Large-size Octagonal	Green/White* Dark Blue	Beige/Pumpkin Light Blue
Cereal, 3⅜"	$7.00-10.00	$18.00-20.00
**Creamer, closed handle, 1½"	$8.00-10.00	$12.00-14.00
**Cup, closed handle, 1½"	$5.00-8.00	***$12.00-15.00
Plate, 4¼"	$3.00-4.00	$8.00-9.00
Saucer, 3⅜"	$2.00-3.00	$4.00-6.00
**Sugar and Lid, closed handle, 1½"	$10.00-14.00	$15.00-18.00
**Teapot and Lid, closed handle, 3⅝"	$16.00-18.00	$20.00-30.00
Boxed Set, 17 pieces	$75.00-100.00	
Boxed Set, 21 pieces	$100.00-140.00	

Large-size Octagonal	Lemonade & Oxblood	Pink/Yellow Other Opaques
Cereal, 3⅜"	$25.00-27.00	$10.00-14.00
Creamer, closed handle, 1½"	$27.00-30.00	$8.00-10.00
Cup, closed handle, 1½"	$22.00-25.00	$8.00-10.00
Plate, 4¼"	$12.00-14.00	$4.50-6.50
Saucer, 3⅜"	$5.00-6.00	$3.00-4.00
Sugar and Lid, closed handle, 1½"	$45.00-50.00	$10.00-14.00
Teapot and Lid, closed handle, 3⅝"	$55.00-65.00	$18.00-20.00
Boxed Set, 17 pieces	$290.00-325.00	$98.00-128.00
Boxed Set, 21 pieces	$395.00-450.00	$140.00-185.00

*With decal, add 50%; **Open handle, add 25%; ***Pumpkin, $22.50

Octagonal, Small

Small-size "Octagonal" sets have only been found in solid opaque colors. Small-size cups are most commonly found with an open handle, but closed handle cups do exist. If teapots, creamers, and sugars with closed handles exist, they are very hard to find.

The most common boxed set contains 16 pieces – four plates, four cups and saucers, a teapot and lid, a creamer and an open sugar. Another type of boxed set containing 21 pieces has been found. This set contains all of the above pieces plus a pitcher and four tumblers.

Since they measure the same, a problem exists among dealers and collectors in distinguishing between large-size "Octagonal" saucers and small-size dinner plates. To determine the difference, look for a greater degree of curvature toward the center in the saucer than in the dinner plate.

Small-size Octagonal	Dark Green Blue/White	Pumpkin/Yellow Lime Green
Creamer, 1¼"	$14.00-16.00	
*Cup, 1¼"	$8.00-10.00	$25.00-27.00
Pitcher, 2¾"	$15.00-18.00	
Plate, 3⅜"	$4.00-6.50	$5.00-6.00
Saucer, 2¾"	$3.00-3.50	$3.00-3.50
Sugar, no Lid, 1¼"	$14.00-16.00	
Teapot and Lid, 3⅜"	$18.00-20.00	
Tumbler, 2"	$10.00-12.00	$18.00-20.00
Boxed Set, 16 pieces	$107.00-140.00	
Boxed Set, 21 pieces	$155.00-198.00	

*Cup, closed handle, add 25%; pumpkin, $10.00-12.00

Raised Daisy

"Raised Daisy" gets its name from the raised floral design found on many of the pieces. A few pieces of "Raised Daisy" shaped glassware without the embossing have been found included in boxed sets. A blue tumbler without a pattern was found enclosed in an unusual 19-piece set. Beige tumblers and yellow tumblers will be found with embossing. Embossed "Raised Daisy" pieces have also been found with interior paneling. Not many of these strange pieces have surfaced yet, but one four-place set is about completed.

Boxed sets in this pattern consist of sets with seven, 13 or 19 pieces. Two different seven-piece sets may be found. One consists of a pitcher and six tumblers. The other set has two dinner plates, two cups and saucers, and an open teapot. The 13-piece set contains four plates, four cups and saucers, and an open teapot. The 19-piece set has four plates, four cups and saucers, an open teapot, a creamer and sugar, and four tumblers.

"Raised Daisy" teapots come in several styles. Of the two lidless styles, only one is embossed. The unembossed one is slightly smaller and thinner, however both types have been found boxed as a lemonade pitcher and a teapot. The third style is shown in the center of the picture. This teapot has a lid which appears to be similar to the "Stacked Disc" teapot lid. However, the lid is unique since it will not interchange with either of the other two "Raised Daisy" teapots or the "Stacked Disc" teapots.

Notice all of the blank areas in the pricing section and you can quickly determine that each piece will only be found in one or two colors. Expect to find sugars and creamers in yellow. Cups will usually be green, but may also be found in blue. Plates are a deep blue and tumblers are normally either yellow or beige.

Raised Daisy	Yellow	Blue	Green	Beige
Creamer, 1¹³/₁₆"	$45.00-50.00			
Cup, 1¹³/₁₆"		$40.00-45.00	$15.00-18.00	
Plate, 3"		$10.00-14.00		
Saucer, 2½"	$8.00-10.00			$8.00-9.00
Sugar, 1¹³/₁₆"	$45.00-50.00			
*Teapot, 2⅜"	$40.00-45.00	$35.00-40.00	$30.00-35.00	
Tumbler, 2"	$25.00-27.00	$55.00-60.00		$30.00-35.00

*Teapot and Lid, blue, $75.00-85.00

Stacked Disc

"Stacked Disc" sets are all small-size. Therefore, the sugar has no lid and there are no cereal bowls to this set. Pieces in the "Stacked Disc" pattern all contain a series of evenly spaced wide horizontal ridges. "Stacked Disc" differs from "Stacked Disc and Interior Panel" since it has a smooth interior surface on the cup, sugar, creamer, teapot, and teapot lid. Also the top surface of the plates and saucers are smooth in "Stacked Disc."

Opaque green and white are the most commonly found colors. There is a limited range of other opaque colors. Pumpkin is probably the most interesting color, but few pieces are found in that color. Supplies in this pattern are adequate for the demand and prices are remaining very reasonable. Therefore this is a good set for beginning collectors to concentrate on.

"Stacked Disc" teapots, creamers, and sugars were also used in "Concentric Rib" sets.

Small-size Stacked Disc	Opaque Green White	Other Opaque Colors
Creamer, 1¼"	$8.00-10.00	*$12.00-14.00
Cup, 1¼"	$4.00-6.00	$10.00-12.00
Pitcher, 2⅞"	$12.00-14.00	$14.00-16.00
Plate, 3¼"	$2.00-3.00	$4.00-5.00
Saucer, 2¾"	$2.00-3.00	$3.00-4.00
Sugar, no Lid, 1¼"	$8.00-10.00	*$12.00-14.00
Teapot and Lid, 3⅜"	$12.50-15.00	*$14.00-16.00
Tumbler, 2"	$7.50-8.50	*$12.00-14.00
Boxed Set, 21 pieces	$105.00-130.00	$170.00-195.00

*Pumpkin, 50% higher

Stacked Disc and Interior Panel, Large

"Stacked Disc and Interior Panel" pattern pieces are a combination of the styles of Akro's two other patterns – "Stacked Disc" and "Interior Panel." Pieces of this pattern have vertical ribs on the interior and horizontal ridges on the exterior. Cereal bowls have the inside panels and a single horizontal ridge on the outside.

The brightly colored opaque sets are popular among collectors and the price for these sets reflects the demand.

Large-size sets have a cereal bowl and sugar lid available. Teapots, creamers, sugars, and lids of this style were also used in the "Concentric Ring" sets.

Stacked Disc & Interior Panel, Large	Solid Opaque Colors	Transparent Green
Cereal, 3⅜"	$20.00-25.00	$20.00-22.00
Creamer, 1⅜"	$22.00-25.00	$25.00-27.00
Cup, 1⅜"	$20.00-22.00	$18.00-20.00
Plate, 4¾"	$10.00-12.00	$10.00-12.00
Saucer, 3¼"	$5.00-6.00	$6.00-7.00
Sugar and Lid, 1⅞"	$32.00-35.00	$35.00-40.00
Teapot and Lid, 3¾"	$45.00-50.00	$45.00-55.00
Boxed Set, 21 pieces	$327.00-370.00	$320.00-370.00

Stacked Disc and Interior Panel, Large-size

Blue marbleized pieces are expecially hard-to-find and locating cobalt cereal bowls, sugars, and creamers is becoming increasingly difficult.

Stacked Disc & Interior Panel, Large	Blue Marbleized	Transparent Cobalt
Cereal, 3⅜"	$40.00-45.00	$28.00-30.00
Creamer, 1⅜"	$35.00-45.00	$30.00-32.00
Cup, 1⅜"	$35.00-40.00	$20.00-25.00
Plate, 4¾"	$18.00-20.00	$14.00-15.00
Saucer, 3¼"	$10.00-12.00	$8.00-10.00
Sugar and Lid, 1⅞"	$50.00-60.00	$50.00-55.00
Teapot and Lid, 3¾"	$95.00-110.00	$70.00-75.00
Boxed Set, 21 pieces	$590.00-685.00	$423.00-475.00

Stacked Disc and Interior Panel, Small-size

Stacked Disc and Interior Panel, Small

As with the large-size sets of the same name, these pieces have vertical ribs on the interior and horizontal ridges on their exterior.

Small-size sets of Akro Agate children's dishes do not contain cereal bowls and the sugars do not have lids. However, a water pitcher and tumbler are available with some sets. Pitchers and tumblers are readily found in the Transoptic colors. Diligent searching will be required to find any tumblers in the solid opaque colors and no opaque colored pitchers have been seen. Neither a pitcher nor tumblers has surfaced in the blue marbleized color. Some people who collect depression glass confuse the tumblers in this pattern with Anchor Hocking's "Block Optic" pattern. Anchor Hocking made no children's dishes in that pattern and the blocks of their small shot glasses are much larger than those in these tumblers.

There also is some problem in distinguishing the water pitcher from a lidless teapot. The interior panels of the teapot bottom continue to the top edge. The pitcher has a ⅞" band around the top which does not have any vertical panels and also lacks the five vertical darts found on the top center of each side of the teapot bottom.

The teapot, creamer, and sugar to this set serve a dual purpose. They are also used with the "Concentric Ring" sets. This dual function has caused some shortages in the supply of these pieces.

Stacked Disc and Interior Panel, Small-size

Stacked Disc & Interior Panel, Small	Solid Opaque Colors	Blue Marbleized	Transparent Green	Transparent Cobalt
Creamer, 1¼"	$16.00-18.00	$40.00-45.00	$25.00-28.00	$35.00-45.00
Cup, 1¼"	$10.00-12.00	$35.00-37.00	$12.00-15.00	$20.00-22.00
Pitcher, 2⅞"			$14.00-18.00	$25.00-27.00
Plate, 3¼"	$4.00-8.00	$18.00-20.00	$7.00-9.00	$12.00-14.00
Saucer, 2¾"	$4.00-5.00	$12.00-14.00	$5.00-8.00	$6.00-8.00
Sugar, 1¼"	$16.00-18.00	$40.00-45.00	$25.00-28.00	$35.00-45.00
Teapot and Lid, 3⅜"	$25.00-35.00	$100.00-125.00	$30.00-35.00	$40.00-50.00
Tumbler, 2"	$40.00-50.00		$12.00-14.00	$15.00-18.00
Boxed Set, 7-piece water			$80.00-100.00	$105.00-132.00
Boxed Set, 8 pieces	$60.00-85.00	$230.00-267.00	$80.00-100.00	$110.00-135.00
Boxed Set, 16 pieces	$170.00-220.00	$440.00-500.00	$175.00-220.00	$260.00-300.00

Stippled Band, Large

Pieces of "Stippled Band" are entirely smooth except for a narrow raised band of dots near the outer exterior surface of each piece. Large-size sets may be found in the transparent blue, green, and amber colors. The color of the amber pieces may vary, and it is difficult to piece these sets together and match the colors. A few pieces in transparent red have been found, but this color is extremely rare and it is suspected that children's pieces in this color may have been produced by workers for their own use.

Only a few cereal bowls, which are normally present in large-size sets, have been found. They are shown below and have only been found in green. They may have been experimental pieces, since they have not been found included in any of the boxed sets. The sugar does have a lid, but it is an unusual size since it will not interchange with the small-size teapot as the sugar lids from other sets will.

Large-size Stippled Band	Transparent Amber	Transparent Green	Transparent Azure
Creamer, 1½"	$20.00-22.00	$20.00-22.00	$28.00-32.00
Cup, 1½"	$10.00-12.00	$6.00-8.00	$20.00-25.00
Plate, 4¼"	$7.00-8.50	$4.50-6.00	$14.00-16.00
Saucer, 3¼"	$5.00-6.00	$2.00-2.50	$10.00-12.00
Sugar and Lid, 1⅞"	$25.00-30.00	$22.00-27.00	$45.00-50.00
Teapot and Lid, 3¾"	$35.00-40.00	$35.00-40.00	$65.00-75.00
Boxed Set, 17 pieces	$167.00-197.00	$130.00-160.00	$315.00-360.00

Stippled Band cereal bowls and unusual style flared tumbler

Stippled Band, Small

A small band of raised dots near the top edge on the exterior surface of each piece is characteristic of the "Stippled Band" pattern. These sets are only found in the Trans-optic colors. The common colors are green and several shades of amber. Some transparent deep red pieces exist, but they are so rare and their color varies so greatly that they were probably experimental. The flared tumbler shown in the photo on the previous page is also probably experimental. Pieces like this are a nice addition to collection of the fortunate owner. Unfortunately, most of us will never have the opportunity for ownership and have to derive our satisfaction from looking at pictures.

Various sizes of boxed sets may be found. Two of the more common sets are the seven-piece water set and the small eight-piece tea set. A four-place boxed set with 16 pieces was also sold. An unusual boxed combination containing a six-place service has also been found. This set consists of 28 pieces and includes a teapot and lid, creamer, sugar, six plates, six cups and saucers, and six tumblers.

Occasionally, "Interior Panel" pieces may be found with stippling. Most collectors do not recognize this "Stippled Interior Panel" variation as a separate pattern and pieces with this dual design are generally collected and priced as if they were "Interior Panel" pattern.

Small-size Stippled Band	Transparent Amber	Transparent Green
Creamer, 1¼"	$25.00-30.00	$25.00-30.00
Cup, 1¼"	$6.00-8.00	$5.00-6.50
Pitcher, 2⅞"	$16.00-18.00	$12.00-14.50
Plate, 3¼"	$4.00-6.00	$3.00-4.00
Saucer, 2¾"	$2.00-2.50	$2.00-2.50
Sugar, no Lid, 1¼"	$25.00-30.00	$25.00-30.00
Teapot and Lid, 3⅜"	$20.00-22.00	$18.00-20.00
Tumbler, 1¾"	$9.00-11.00	$8.00-10.00
Boxed Set, 7 pieces	$70.00-78.00	$55.00-70.00
Boxed Set, 8 pieces	$45.00-55.00	$40.00-47.00
Boxed Set, 16 pieces	$115.00-145.00	$105.00-130.00
Boxed Set, 28 pieces	$165.00-200.00	$142.00-175.00

Glasbake "Betty Jane Baking Set" (McKee Glass Co.)

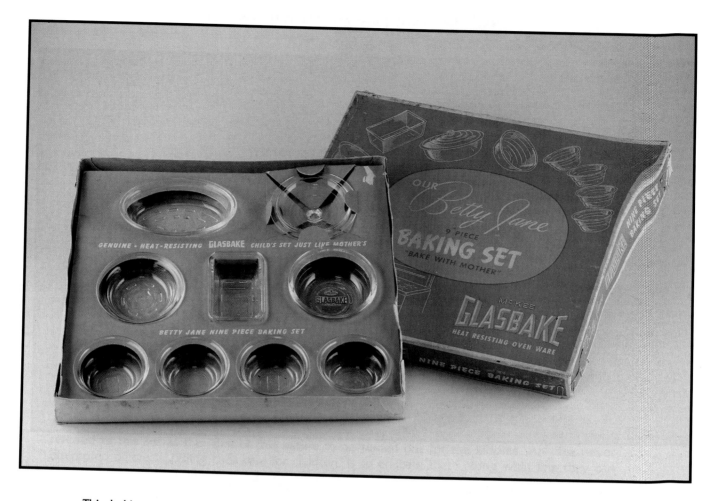

This baking set consists of nine pieces of heat resisting ovenware. Sets such as these were designed for a child to use while baking along with mother. The #58 bowl was also used as an adult-size custard and has little value outside of the boxed set. Many sets with purple flashing may have an undesirable mottled appearance. This appearance results from damage to the flashing which occurs if the pieces have been played with extensively.

	Crystal
Baker, oval (075), 4¼" x 6⅜"	$10.00-12.00
Bowl, (58), 3⅝"	$1.50-2.50
Bread Baker, (025), 3" x 4½"	$10.00-12.00
Casserole, covered, (064), 3⅛"	$25.00-27.00
Pie Plate, (97), 4½"	$10.00-12.00
Boxed Set, 9 pieces	$60.00-70.00

Flashed Set, add 20%

Fire King "Sunny Suzy Baking Set No. 260" (Anchor Hocking)

This seven-piece Fire King baking set was made for the Wolverine Supply & Mfg. Company in the late 1940's. None of the pieces in this set were made as special children's pieces. The set utilizes regular adult-size Fire King pieces consisting of four 5 oz. custard cups, a 5⅜" cereal bowl, and an individual 10 oz. covered casserole. All these light blue-colored glass pieces are found frequently and the true value of this set to a collector of children's dishes is in obtaining this set with an original box.

Casserole, covered, 10 oz.	$8.00-10.00
Custard Cup, 5 oz.	$2.00-2.50
Dish, deep pie, 5⅜"	$14.00-16.00
Boxed Set, 7 pieces	$100.00-125.00

Fire King "Sunny Suzy Baking Set No. 261" (Anchor Hocking)

This delightful little set was made for the Wolverine Supply and Manufacturing Company during the 1940's. The light blue-colored glass pieces were made by Anchor Hocking. Since they used the same pieces from their regular baking line, collectors of children's dishes are only interested in boxed sets. This set is shown in a 1946 Spiegel catalog.

Baker, 2-handle, 10 oz.	$8.00-10.00
Custard Cup, 5 oz.	$2.00-2.50
Dish, deep pie, 5⅜"	$14.00-16.00
Pastry Board	$4.00-6.00
Rolling Pin	$10.00-12.00
Boxed Set, 8 pieces	$105.00-130.00

The Pyrexette Bakeware Set

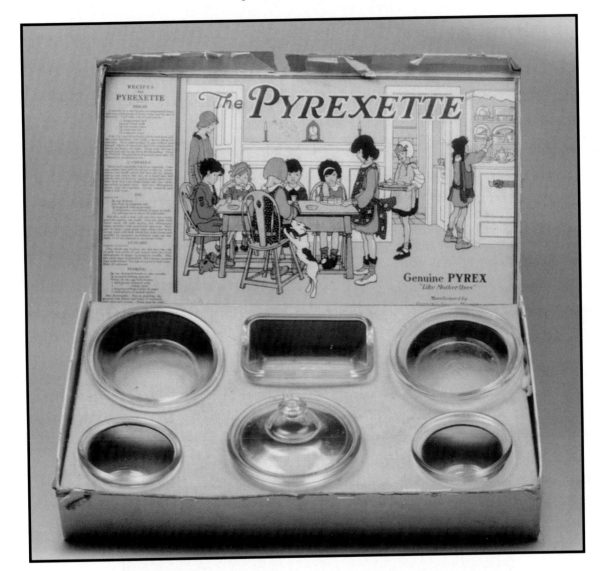

This Bakeware set consists of a bread baker, a pie plate, a covered casserole, and two custard dishes. The custards are the same as the ones used in the adult set. The set was made by the Corning Glass Works of Corning, New York. Recipes for the young Pyrexette are included on the inside of the box top.

Bread Baker, 3" x 4¾"	$20.00-22.00
Casserole and Cover, 4½"	$25.00-30.00
Custard, 3½"	$1.50-2.50
Pie Plate, 5"	$16.00-18.00
Boxed Set	$150.00-175.00

Miscellaneous Depression Era Items

The above items were made in the 1930's and 1940's. The child's mixer is marked "Delta Detroit." The mixing bowls used with it are Glasbake by McKee.

The hand beater on the left is Glasbake. The same base was also used as an egg cup. The beater on the right is marked "Betty Taplin."

The remainder of the pieces in the picture are part of a "Little Deb" series. The ribbed bowl in the foreground is inscribed "Little Deb Toys" and was probably a promotional item. The tumblers, tray, and pitcher comprise a lemonade set. The glass pieces of this set (a regular-size creamer and adult-size shot glass) were made by Hazel Atlas for the Northwestern Products Company. This set was sold as the "Little Deb Lemonade Set No. 207." Retail price in a 1946 *Spiegel* catalog was 89 cents.

A "Little Deb" toaster set is pictured in the photo below. It was sold with a metal tray and four crystal "Little Deb" bowls.

Beater, Glasbake, 6⅜"	$35.00-40.00	Pitcher, 3⅞"	$5.00-6.00
Beater, Betty Taplin, 6⅛"	$50.00-60.00	Tumbler, 2⅛"	$3.00-4.00
Bowl, Glasbake, 3⅝"	$8.00-10.00	Boxed Lemonade Set	$45.00-55.00
Bowl, Ribbed Little Deb, 3⅛"	$15.00-18.00	Boxed Toaster Set	$75.00-95.00
Mixer, Delta Detroit, 5"	$30.00-40.00		

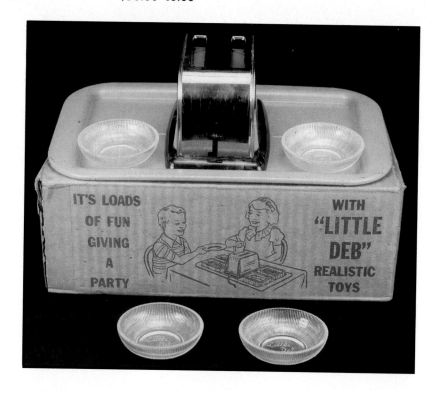

"LITTLE DEB" APPLIANCE SET--NON-ELECTRIC

Appliances for a play-house kitchen that will make even a grownup wish she were six again! Two-slice Pop-up Toaster in chrome and metal, with attached cord . . . metal Mixer in Red and White enamel finish, with white milk glass bowl, attached cord . . . chrome Waffle Baker, with colorful plastic mixing bowl and syrup pitcher, metal tray . . . Pink Lemonade set, consisting of a clear glass pitcher, four glasses, handled serving tray with wonderland figures on it.
81204 B400 Retail Price. Set $5.75

From The John Plain Book, 1949

Little Deb Mixer $40.00-50.00

Miniature Sunbeam Mixmaster with
Jadite Bowls
$150.00-185.00

Miniature Beater, left $50.00-75.00
Miniature Beater, center $45.00-55.00
Miniature Tumble-up $35.00-45.00

Jadite Canister Set (Jeannette Glass Co.)

Jeannette's regular-size spice canisters were also used to produce a child's canister set. This was accomplished by merely changing the labels of the spice canisters. The result was the five-piece miniature canister set shown in the picture.

Canister, 3" $100.00-110.00

Toddy Chocolate Set

This boxed child's chocolate set was marketed by Toddy, Inc. of Rochester, New York. It includes a sample tin of chocolate mix, an aluminum shaker, four pink Hazel Atlas tumblers, four spoons, four cloth napkins, and four straws. The tumblers are 2⅜" high; the shaker is 5" tall; and the spoons are 3" long.

Boxed Chocolate Set
$100.00-125.00

Lemonade Set (Mirro Aluminum)

Mirro Aluminum Toys sold this miniature lemonade set. The original retail price was $1.00. The set consists of a 4½" aluminum pitcher, six crystal 2¼" Hocking "Block Optic" tumblers, and an 8" aluminum serving tray.

Boxed Lemonade Set $60.00-75.00

Little Tots Tea Set (England)

This crudely fashioned, clear green glass, set consists of three cups and saucers, an open handless sugar, a creamer, and a covered teapot. The box identifies it as one of the "CODEG Series, Made in England." It probably dates from the 1950's.

Creamer, 1⅜"	$8.00-10.00
Cup, 1½"	$5.00-6.00
Saucer, 3⅜"	$2.00-3.00
Sugar, 1⅛"	$8.00-10.00
Teapot and Lid, 3¾"	$12.00-14.00
Boxed Set	$50.00-60.00

Blown Miniatures and Port Set

Jug, Cobalt, 1¼" $30.00-35.00
Jug, Floral, 2" $30.00-35.00
Jug, Orange Swirl, 1½" $27.00-30.00
Jug, Tall, 3" $30.00-35.00
Jug, Yellow Stripe, 1½" $27.00-32.00
Urn, Red, 1¼" $25.00-30.00

Port Set: Tray, 2" x 3½"
Decanter, 1¾"; tumbler, ¾" $35.00-40.00

Pattern Glass Children's Dishes

Pressed glass toy dishes were produced by many glass houses during the last half of the 19th century and in the early years of the 20th century. Several events combined in the late 1800's to promote the popularity of pressed glass. The process of pressing glass into a mold was perfected; abundant supplies of cheap natural glass became available in western Pennsylvania, eastern Ohio, and West Virginia; and calcium oxide replaced lead oxide as an ingredient in the glass formula. The result was a low melting mixture that was easily shaped. The end product was inexpensive, but durable.

The various companies produced several basic types of miniature sets. Included in these were table sets, water sets, punch sets, berry sets, vegetable sets, and stein sets. A table set consists of a covered butter, a covered sugar, a creamer, and a spooner. The punch set includes a punch bowl and six small punch cups. The water set has a pitcher and six tumblers. The berry set consists of one large berry and six small berries. The vegetable set is shown in a Federal Glass Company catalog. It is only known in the "Tulip and Honeycomb" pattern and is composed of four pieces. Included are a round covered dish, an oval covered dish, a round open dish, and an oval open dish. Stein sets are composed of a master stein and six small steins. Other special pieces such as candlesticks, mugs, or cups and saucers were made in a few of the tableware patterns. These accessory items may also be found in many other patterns.

The Sandwich glass shown on page 109 was made by the Sandwich Glass Company of Sandwich, Massachusetts. The "lacy" miniatures were produced between 1825 and 1840. When demand for this type of glass dropped, the company started producing "paneled" pieces. These were made until 1888, when the company closed. Several attempts were made to reopen the factory between 1888 and 1900, but none were successful.

Acorn

All four pieces feature an acorn on their footed base. The sugar creamer and spooner have Kate Greenway type children inside ovals on their sides.

	Crystal	**Crystal Frosted**
Butter, 4"	$250.00-300.00	$300.00-350.00
Creamer, 3⅜"	$100.00-110.00	$200.00-250.00
Spooner, 3⅛"	$100.00-110.00	$175.00-200.00
Sugar and Lid, 4¾"	$150.00-200.00	$200.00-250.00
Table Set	$600.00-720.00	$875.00-1,050.00

Arched Panel (Westmoreland Glass Co.)

Arched Panel was listed as Westmoreland's No. 304 water set in their catalogs. Depression glass collectors may know this set by the name "Little Jo" from Hazel Weatherman's reference. Original production included crystal, light green, light pink, and deep amber colors. The set is commonly found in crystal, but is elusive in old colors. Westmoreland reissued this set in 1977. It was produced for LeVay Distributing under the name Flute. New colors included amberina, cobalt, crystal, green, red carnival, green carnival, cobalt carnival, cobalt with white hand-painted flowers, green with hand-painted white flowers, and crystal with hand-painted blue and white flowers.

	Crystal	Amber	**Pink/Green Cobalt
Pitcher, 3¾"	$30.00-35.00	$84.00-96.00	$110.00-120.00
Tumbler, 2"	$6.00-8.00	$20.00-22.00	$27.00-30.00
*Water Set, 7 pieces	$66.00-83.00	$204.00-228.00	$272.00-300.00

*Reproduced in crystal and colors
**Prices for original production pieces only

Austrian No. 200 (Greentown)

	Crystal	Canary	Chocolate
Butter, 2¼"	$185.00-200.00	$300.00-350.00	$750.00-800.00
Creamer, 3¼"	$75.00-85.00	$175.00-200.00	$300.00-325.00
Spooner, 3"	$90.00-110.00	$175.00-200.00	$300.00-350.00
Sugar and Lid, 3¾"	$150.00-175.00	$275.00-300.00	$500.00-550.00
Table Set	$500.00-570.00	$925.00-1,050.00	$1,850.00-2,025.00

Baby Thumbprint
(United States Glass Co.)

A butter dish has been found listed in a 1915 United States Glass Company catalog. The large cakestand has a single row of elongated oval embossing and the small comport has a double row of pattern. The comport with the flared rim does not have a cover.

	Crystal
Butter, 3"	ND
Cakestand, tall, 3"	$90.00-110.00
Cakestand, short, 2"	$100.00-125.00
Compote, covered, 4"	$150.00-175.00
Compote, flared rim (no cover)	$175.00-200.00

Bead and Scroll

Dark green, dark blue, and amber pieces do exist, but are lacking from many collections. Also some pieces, especially creamers, are found red-flashed over crystal and adorned with the names of people or vacation spots.

	*Crystal	**Dark Green Blue/Amber**
Butter, 4"	$175.00-195.00	$275.00-300.00
Creamer, 3"	$70.00-80.00	$100.00-120.00
Spooner, 2¾"	$70.00-80.00	$120.00-140.00
Sugar and Lid, 4"	$100.00-125.00	$130.00-160.00
Table Set	$425.00-480.00	$625.00-720.00

*With gold trim or red flashing, add 10%

Beaded Swirl (Westmoreland Glass Co.)

Crystal pieces of this pattern are fairly abundant. Completing a set in any color is a real challenge.

	Crystal	Amber Cobalt
Butter, 2⅜"	$47.00-52.00	$125.00-150.00
Creamer, 2¾"	$27.00-30.00	$80.00-90.00
Spooner, 2¼"	$30.00-40.00	$120.00-150.00
Sugar and Lid, 3¾"	$39.00-42.00	$100.00-125.00
Table Set	$143.00-164.00	$425.00-515.00

Block

This set is similar in appearance to McKee's Tappan Set. However, there are marked differences. In the Tappan pattern there are alternating smooth and waffle-like blocks, while the squares of the "Block" pattern are smooth. Also the edge of the "Block" butter bottom is scalloped while the edge of the Tappan butter bottom is smooth and the shape of the handles of the creamers is different.

	Crystal	Amber	Blue
Butter, 3"	$150.00-175.00	$165.00-185.00	$165.00-185.00
*Creamer, 3"	$50.00-60.00	$60.00-70.00	$60.00-70.00
Spooner, 3"	$80.00-100.00	$90.00-110.00	$95.00-120.00
Sugar and Lid, 4½"	$110.00-130.00	$125.00-150.00	$125.00-150.00
Table Set	$390.00-465.00	$440.00-515.00	$445.00-525.00

*Blue milk glass $100.00-125.00

Braided Belt

Braided Belt is a four-piece table set. It is normally found with hand-painted half-flower decorations, but these are subject to wear with use and some pieces may be found with the decoration missing.

	Crystal	White/ Decorated	Amber Light Green
Butter, 2¼"	$120.00-150.00	$270.00-300.00	$310.00-340.00
Creamer, 2⅝"	$70.00-85.00	$100.00-115.00	$120.00-140.00
Spooner, 2⅝"	$70.00-90.00	$100.00-120.00	$130.00-150.00
Sugar and Lid, 3½"	$90.00-110.00	$180.00-210.00	$190.00-220.00
Table Set	$350.00-435.00	$650.00-745.00	$750.00-850.00

Bucket or "Wooden Pail" (Bryce Brothers)

Bucket is also sometimes referred to as "Wooden Pail." It is difficult to find and has only been seen in crystal.

	Crystal
Butter, 2¼"	$260.00-280.00
Creamer, 2½"	$50.00-60.00
Spooner, 2½"	$160.00-180.00
Sugar and Lid, 3¾"	$175.00-200.00
Table Set	$645.00-720.00

Button Panel No. 44 (George Duncan's Sons)

	Crystal	**Crystal/Gold**
Butter, 4"	$85.00-95.00	$90.00-100.00
Creamer, 2½"	$47.00-52.00	$52.00-57.00
Spooner, 2⁹/₁₆"	$57.00-62.00	$60.00-67.00
Sugar and Lid, 4⅝"	$80.00-90.00	$85.00-95.00
Table Set	$270.00-300.00	$285.00-320.00

Buzz Saw No. 2697 (Cambridge Glass Co.)

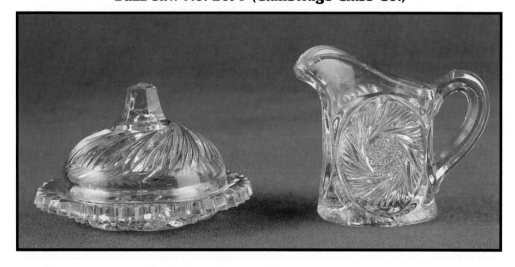

This table set was advertised by Cambridge as "near cut" but is crude in appearance. As the relatively inexpensive prices below indicate, all pieces are relatively common and supplies are adequate.

	Crystal
Butter, 2⅜"	$30.00-35.00
Creamer, 2⅜"	$22.00-25.00
Spooner, 2⅛"	$22.00-25.00
Sugar and Lid, 2⅞"	$30.00-32.00
Table Set	$104.00-117.00

Chimo

Beware of new spooners and creamers which have been reproduced in crystal and colors by L.E. Smith.

	Crystal
Butter, 2⅜"	$100.00-125.00
*Creamer, 2"	$40.00-50.00
*Spooner, 2⅛"	$50.00-60.00
Sugar and Lid, 3"	$70.00-90.00
Table Set	$260.00-325.00
Punch Cup, 1⁷⁄₁₆"	$16.00-18.00

*Reproduced in both crystal and colors.

Clear and Diamond Panel

Note two sizes of butters may be found for this table set.

	Crystal	Green	Blue
Butter, 2⅞"	$45.00-55.00	$60.00-65.00	$65.00-70.00
Butter, 4"	$60.00-65.00	$110.00-130.00	$125.00-150.00
Creamer, 2¾"	$20.00-22.00	$32.00-37.00	$37.00-40.00
Spooner, 2¼"	$22.00-25.00	$32.00-37.00	$37.00-40.00
Sugar and Lid, 3½"	$35.00-40.00	$42.00-47.00	$50.00-55.00
Table Set	$122.00-137.00	$175.00-190.00	$185.00-205.00

Cloud Band (Gillinder and Sons, Inc.)

	Crystal	**Decorated White Milk Glass**
Butter, 3¾"	$110.00-125.00	$165.00-185.00
Creamer, 2½"	$40.00-45.00	$55.00-65.00
Spooner, 2⅜"	$40.00-45.00	$65.00-75.00
Sugar and Lid, 4"	$70.00-80.00	$100.00-120.00
Table Set	$260.00-295.00	$385.00-445.00

Colonial Flute

	Crystal		**Crystal**
Pitcher, 3¼"	$18.00-22.00	Punch Bowl, 3³⁄₁₆"	$40.00-50.00
Tumbler, 2"	$4.00-5.00	Punch Cup, 1⅞"	$13.00-14.00
Water Set, 7 pieces	$42.00-52.00	Punch Set, 7 pieces	$118.00-134.00

The berry set to the Colonial Flute pattern is similar to another berry set called Flute. The easiest way to distinguish between the two patterns is to look at the rays in the bottom of the bowls. Flute has rays of equal length while the rays in the Colonial Flute pieces are uneven.

	Crystal	**Crystal w/ Gold**
Master Berry, 2"	$22.00-25.00	$47.00-52.00
Small Berry, 1"	$6.50-7.50	$20.00-25.00
Berry Set, 7 pieces	$61.00-70.00	$167.00-200.00

Colonial No. 2630 (Cambridge Glass Co.)

Cambridge Colonial is one of the easier sets for collectors to find in color. Finding colored sets with all the pieces that match perfectly is somewhat of a problem. Sometimes pieces in sets which are bought complete will be slightly different shades.

	Crystal	Olive & Emerald Green	Cobalt
Butter, 2½"	$22.00-25.00	$47.00-52.00	$50.00-55.00
Creamer, 2⅜"	$15.00-17.00	$30.00-35.00	$35.00-40.00
Spooner, 2⅛"	$19.00-22.00	$35.00-40.00	$40.00-45.00
Sugar and Lid, 3"	$20.00-25.00	$40.00-45.00	$45.00-50.00
Table Set	$78.00-89.00	$150.00-170.00	$170.00-190.00

Dewdrop or "Hobnail with Hobnail Base" (Columbia Glass Co.)

Factory J of the U.S. Glass combine (Columbia Glass Company of Findlay, Ohio) produced this pattern child's set in the last decade of the 1800's.

	Crystal	Blue Amber
Butter, 2⅝"	$125.00-150.00	$150.00-170.00
Creamer, 2¾"	$50.00-60.00	$60.00-70.00
Spooner, 2¾"	$60.00-70.00	$70.00-80.00
Sugar and Lid, 4⅛"	$85.00-95.00	$100.00-110.00
Table Set	$320.00-375.00	$380.00-420.00

Diamond Ridge or "D&M No. 48" (George Duncan & Sons)

	Crystal
Butter	$180.00-195.00
Creamer, 2½"	$75.00-85.00
Spooner, 2¾"	$95.00-110.00
Sugar and Lid, 4⅝"	$130.00-150.00
Table Set	$480.00-540.00

Doyle No. 500 (Doyle and Co.)

This interesting set was produced by Doyle and Company of Pittsburgh, Pennsylvania in the late 1880's. The set is unusual in that it is one of only a few pattern glass children's sets with a tray.

	Crystal	***Amber**	**Blue**
Butter, 2¼"	$70.00-80.00	$90.00-110.00	$125.00-150.00
Creamer, 2½"	$35.00-40.00	$60.00-65.00	$70.00-75.00
Spooner, 2¼"	$40.00-45.00	$65.00-70.00	$75.00-80.00
Sugar and Lid, 3⅝"	$50.00-55.00	$75.00-85.00	$95.00-110.00
Tray, 6⅝"	$27.00-35.00	$60.00-70.00	$70.00-80.00
Table Set	$222.00-255.00	$350.00-400.00	$445.00-495.00
Mug, 2"	$22.00-25.00	$35.00-37.00	$40.00-50.00

*Canary, add 20%

Drum

Drum is a four-piece table set which was produced in crystal. In addition, there are three different sizes of crystal mugs. The mug which measures 2³/₁₆" high has been reproduced.

	Crystal		Crystal
Butter, 2¼"	$100.00-125.00	*Mug, 2³/₁₆"	$18.00-20.00
Creamer, 2¾"	$62.00-67.00	Mug, 2½"	$29.00-32.00
Spooner, 2⅝"	$67.00-70.00	Mug, 2"	$35.00-40.00
Sugar and Lid, 3½"	$100.00-110.00	Table Set	$329.00-372.00
*Reproduced			

D&M No. 42 (George Duncan & Sons)

	*Crystal		*Crystal
Butter, 4"	$150.00-175.00	Table Set	$325.00-375.00
Creamer, 2⅝"	$45.00-50.00	Honey Jug, 2⅜"	$60.00-65.00
Spooner, 2⁹/₁₆"	$50.00-55.00	Rose Bowl, 2⅛"	$67.00-75.00
Sugar and Lid, 4½"	$80.00-95.00		
*Gold decorated, add 10%			

Dutch Boudoir

Dutch Boudoir is an example of a chamber set. Notice the two pomade jars and a single candle rest nicely on the tray. Both the slop jar and the potty will be found with glass lids and the pomade has a metal cover. Candlesticks have been reproduced since 1987, by Mosser Glass Company of Cambridge, Ohio. They are currently available in blue milk glass, but may appear in other colors. The new candles have an "M" on the base.

	White Milk Glass	**Blue Milk Glass**
Bowl, 1³/₁₆"	$85.00-90.00	$110.00-120.00
*Candlestick, 3"	$75.00-80.00	$110.00-125.00
Chamber Pot and Lid, 2⅛"	$95.00-110.00	$125.00-135.00
Pitcher, 2¼"	$85.00-95.00	$115.00-130.00
**Pomade, 1½"	$100.00-125.00	$115.00-135.00
Slop Jar and Lid, 2⅜"	$110.00-130.00	$130.00-140.00
Tray, 3¼" x 6"	$140.00-160.00	$165.00-185.00

*Apple Green, $125.00-135.00   **Crystal, $120.00-130.00

Fernland No. 2635 (Cambridge Glass Co.)

	Crystal	Olive & Emerald Green	Cobalt
Butter, 2⅝"	$22.00-27.00	$50.00-54.00	$55.00-60.00
Creamer, 2⅜"	$18.00-20.00	$35.00-40.00	$37.00-40.00
Spooner, 2⅜"	$19.00-22.00	$35.00-40.00	$37.00-40.00
Sugar and Lid, 3"	$25.00-30.00	$40.00-45.00	$48.00-52.00
Table Set	$84.00-99.00	$155.00-175.00	$165.00-190.00

Hawaiian Lei (J.B. Higbee Glass Co.)

Original sets were made by Higbee in crystal. Mosser Glass Company of Cambridge, Ohio is currently reproducing the butter, sugar, and creamer in both crystal and colors. The Mosser reissues have the Higbee "Bee" trademark on the bottom of each piece, but the letters "HIG" have been removed. The spooner has not been reissued.

	Crystal		**Crystal**
*Butter, 2¼"	$35.00-37.00	*Sugar and Lid, 3"	$27.00-30.00
*Creamer, 2"	$17.00-20.00	Table Set	$103.00-114.00
Spooner, 2¼"	$24.00-27.00	Cakeplate	$45.00-50.00

*Reproduced in crystal, light blue, pink, cobalt, red

Hobnail with Thumbprint Base No. 150 (Doyle and Co.)

	Crystal	**Blue Amber**
Butter, 2"	$67.00-72.00	$110.00-120.00
Creamer, 3⅜"	$35.00-40.00	$45.00-55.00
Spooner, 2⅞"	$42.00-47.00	$70.00-75.00
Sugar and Lid, 4"	$62.00-68.00	$90.00-100.00
Tray, 7⅜"	$30.00-40.00	$50.00-60.00
Table Set	$236.00-267.00	$365.00-$410.00

Horizontal Threads

The Fenton Glass Company of Williamstown, West Virginia now owns these molds. The entire table set has been reproduced in a blue opalescent color since 1990.

	*Crystal
Butter, 1⅞"	$80.00-90.00
Creamer, 2¼"	$35.00-40.00
Spooner, 2⅛"	$40.00-45.00
Sugar and Lid, 3⅜"	$55.00-65.00
Table Set	$210.00-240.00

*Red flashed, add 20%

Ice Cream Cone Ice Cream Set (Federal Glass Co.)
Fish Ice Cream Set

Complete sets consist of six small round plates and one oval platter. The small plates have an alphabet border and the oval platter has a leaf-like design on the border. All pieces are difficult to locate. Shown in the foreground of the photo is a small plate from the Fish Ice Cream Set which was also made by the Federal Glass Company.

	Ice Cream Set	Fish Set
Plate, 2¾"	$40.00-45.00	$85.00-95.00
Platter, 4½" x 5¾"	$140.00-150.00	$300.00-340.00
Set, 7 pieces	$380.00-420.00	$810.00-910.00

Inverted Strawberry (Cambridge Glass Co.)

The punch set has been reproduced by Mosser Glass Company of Cambridge, Ohio. All new pieces are supposed to be marked with an "M," but apparently some are unmarked. However, there are some significant differences between the old and new sets. The old punch bowl has eight large scallops at the top and has four strawberries around the top of the bowl. The new punch bowl only has six large scallops and three strawberries at the top. Strawberries on the old cups are attached to their stems, while the strawberries and stems on the new cups have a slight separation.

	Crystal		**Crystal**
Master Berry, 1⅝"	$60.00-65.00	*Punch Bowl, 3⅜"	$47.00-52.00
Small Berry, ½"	$19.00-22.00	*Punch Cup, 1⅛"	$18.00-20.00
Berry Set	$174.00-197.00	Punch Set	$155.00-172.00

*Reproduced in crystal and colors by Mosser Glass Co.

"Kittens" (Fenton Glass Co.)

Recent issues by Fenton include similarly shaped pieces in aqua, opalescent, and red.

	Marigold	**Blue**
Banana Dish	$135.00-145.00	
Bowl, cereal, 3½"	$100.00-125.00	
Bowl, ruffled, 4 point, 4½"	$110.00-115.00	
Bowl, ruffled, 6 point, 4¼"	$130.00-145.00	
Cup, 2⅛"	$85.00-90.00	$150.00-170.00
Saucer, 4½"	$45.00-50.00	$60.00-65.00
Vase, ruffled, 2⅜"	$165.00-185.00	

Children's Dishes

Lamb

A three-piece table set was reproduced in white milk glass, iridized red, and iridized dark blue by Imperial Glass Company in the early 1980's. These pieces include the covered butter, covered sugar, and creamer. After Imperial closed, the molds were sold and production has continued mostly in iridized colors. The spooner has not been reissued.

	*Crystal		*Crystal
**Butter, 3⅛"	$150.00-175.00	Spooner, 2⅛"	$90.00-110.00
**Creamer, 2⅞"	$62.00-70.00	**Sugar and Lid, 4⅛"	$105.00-120.00
Table Set	$407.00-475.00		

*White milk glass, old, add 50%

**Reproduced in carnival colors and white milk glass.

Liberty Bell

	*Crystal		*Crystal
Butter, 2¼"	$200.00-225.00	Sugar and Lid, 3⅝"	$150.00-175.00
Creamer, 2½"	$75.00-95.00	Table Set	$565.00-645.00
Spooner, 2⅜"	$140.00-150.00	Mug, 2"	$100.00-125.00

*White milk glass, double price

Lion (Gillinder and Sons)

	Crystal	Frosted Crystal	Crystal with Frosted Head
Butter, 4¼"	$90.00-100.00	$135.00-140.00	$160.00-180.00
Creamer, 3⅛"	$62.00-68.00	$75.00-80.00	$85.00-95.00
Spooner, 3"	$82.00-87.00	$90.00-95.00	$100.00-110.00
Sugar and Lid, 4¼"	$90.00-95.00	$110.00-115.00	$120.00-125.00
Table Set	$325.00-350.00	$410.00-425.00	$485.00-510.00
Cup, 1¹¹⁄₁₆"	$35.00-40.00	$40.00-45.00	$50.00-60.00
Saucer, 3¼"	$15.00-20.00	$15.00-20.00	$15.00-20.00

Menagerie (Bryce, Higbee Co.)

The Menagerie table set is comprised of four different animal figures. The spooner is an open mouth fish, the creamer an owl, the covered sugar is a standing bear and a turtle forms the butter. The only confusing piece is the sugar. The same bear figure was also used with an open slot at the top of the base as an adult-size marmalade. Since the slotted figure is more easily found than the actual toy sugar, some collectors are substituting this for the real thing at a reduced price. As the price indicates, the turtle butter is much harder to find than the other pieces to the set.

	Crystal	Amber	Blue
Butter, 2⅜"	$800.00-900.00	$1,200.00-1,400.00	$1,800.00-2,000.00
Creamer, 3¾"	$85.00-95.00	$130.00-140.00	$120.00-135.00
Spooner, 2⅝"	$85.00-95.00	$130.00-140.00	$120.00-135.00
*Sugar & Lid, 4¼"	$240.00-260.00	$350.00-375.00	$325.00-350.00
Table Set	$1,205.00-1,305.00	$1,810.00-2,055.00	$2,365.00-2,620.00

*Sugar lid does not have open slot.

Michigan (U.S. Glass Co.)

In addition to the table set pictured, a Stein Set may also be found. The child's creamer is used as the main stein. The small steins are handled with plain sides, except for verticle ribbing near the bottom. This ribbing covers about the lower quarter of the stein.

	Crystal	Crystal with Gold	Crystal Flashed Red & Green
Butter, 3½"	$90.00-95.00	$115.00-120.00	$140.00-150.00
Creamer, 2⅞"	$37.00-42.00	$50.00-55.00	$65.00-70.00
Spooner, 3"	$37.00-42.00	$50.00-55.00	$65.00-70.00
Sugar and Lid, 4¼"	$64.00-68.00	$80.00-86.00	$105.00-115.00
Table Set	$230.00-250.00	$295.00-315.00	$375.00-400.00

	Crystal	Crystal with Gold
Stein, main, 2⅞"	$37.00-42.00	$50.00-55.00
Stein, small, 2"	$6.00-8.00	$10.00-12.00
Stein Set, 7 places	$72.00-92.00	$110.00-127.00

"Monk" Stein Set

White milk glass pieces may be found flashed with various colors or trimmed with gold. Notice the two different styles shown in the picture. Crystal pieces have only been found with the rings, but milk glass pieces may be found with or without rings. Crystal pieces are less plentiful than white milk glass pieces. Seven-piece sets – six stein and one tankard – wholesaled for 92 cents a dozen in 1914 according to an ad in a Butler Brothers' catalog.

	Crystal	White Milk Glass
Stein, 2"	$27.00-30.00	$22.00-25.00
Tankard, 4"	$70.00-80.00	$55.00-60.00
Set, 5 pieces	$178.00-200.00	$143.00-160.00

Nearcut Water Set (Cambridge Glass Co.)

	Crystal
Pitcher, 3⅛"	$28.00-30.00
Tumbler, 2"	$5.50-6.50
Water Set	$60.00-70.00

Nursery Rhyme (U.S. Glass Co.)

The child's master berry in this set is the same as the adult-size small berry. The table set, berry set, and water set are only available in crystal. The punch set was also produced in transparent blue and blue milk glass, but these colors are hard to find.

	Crystal		Crystal
Butter, 2⅜"	$80.00-100.00	Pitcher, 4¼"	$90.00-110.00
Creamer, 2½"	$45.00-55.00	Tumbler, 2"	$20.00-22.00
Spooner, 2½"	$50.00-60.00	Water Set, 7 pieces	$210.00-242.00
Sugar and Lid, 3⅞"	$70.00-90.00	Master Berry, 1¼" x 4¼"	$85.00-95.00
Table Set	$245.00-305.00	Small Berry, 1¼" x 2½"	$20.00-22.00
Berry Set, 7 pieces	$205.00-227.00		

Nursery Rhyme (U.S. Glass Co.)

	Crystal	White Milk Glass	Blue Milk Glass	Transparent Blue
Punch Bowl, 3¼"	$90.00-120.00	$125.00-135.00	$300.00-350.00	$425.00-475.00
Punch Cup, 1⅜"	$20.00-22.00	$23.00-25.00	$40.00-45.00	$70.00-75.00
Punch Set, 7 pieces	$210.00-252.00	$263.00-285.00	$540.00-620.00	$845.00-925.00

Oval Star No. 300 (Indiana Glass Co.)

The complete water set may consist of 5, 6 or 8 pieces. It was sold with a pitcher, an optional round tray, and either 4 or 6 tumblers. The tray is the hardest piece to find.

	*Crystal		*Crystal
Butter, 3½"	$19.00-21.00	Pitcher, 4"	$55.00-65.00
Creamer, 2½"	$15.00-17.00	Tumbler, 2¼"	$8.00-9.00
Spooner, 2½"	$20.00-22.00	Tray, 7¼"	$80.00-85.00
Sugar and Lid, 4⅜"	$22.00-25.00	Water Set, 8 pieces	$183.00-204.00
Table Set	$78.00-85.00	Master Berry, 2"	$40.00-45.00
Punch Bowl	$52.00-55.00	Small Berry, 1"	$8.00-9.00
Punch Cup	$7.50-8.50	Berry Set, 7 pieces	$88.00-98.00
Punch Set, 7 pieces	$97.00-105.00		
*Crystal with gold, add 25%			

Pattee Cross (U.S. Glass Co.)

	*Crystal		*Crystal
Master Berry, 1¾"	$35.00-40.00	Punch Set, 7 pieces	$205.00-227.00
Small Berry, 1"	$10.00-12.00	Pitcher, 4½"	$60.00-65.00
Berry Set, 7 pieces	$95.00-110.00	Tumbler, 1¾"	$12.00-14.00
Punch Bowl, 2½"	$85.00-95.00	Water Set, 7 pieces	$132.00-149.00
Punch Cup, 1⅛"	$20.00-22.00		
*Crystal with gold, add 25%			

Peacock Feather (U.S. Glass Co.)

	Crystal
Cakestand, 3"	$85.00-95.00
Creamer, 2"	$45.00-50.00

Pennsylvania (U.S. Glass Co.)

Pennsylvania is available as a four-piece table set in crystal or green. Either set is sometimes found trimmed in gold. This is a hard set to complete in green.

	*Crystal	*Green
Butter, 3½"	$95.00-110.00	$195.00-225.00
Creamer, 2½"	$40.00-45.00	$85.00-95.00
Spooner, 2½"	$40.00-45.00	$85.00-95.00
Sugar and Lid, 4"	$65.00-75.00	$150.00-175.00
Table Set	$240.00-270.00	$515.00-590.00

*With gold trim, add 25%

Pert

	Crystal
Butter, 2¾"	$120.00-125.00
Creamer, 3¼"	$80.00-85.00
Spooner, 3"	$120.00-125.00
Sugar and Lid, 5⅛"	$135.00-140.00
Table Set	$455.00-475.00

Plain Pattern No. 13 (King Glass Co.)

This table set may be found in crystal, crystal with frosted panels, white milk glass, and cobalt. It is very hard to find in crystal and very elusive in color.

	*Crystal	White Milk Glass	Cobalt
Butter, 1⅞"	$100.00-125.00	$150.00-175.00	$175.00-200.00
Creamer, 2¼"	$50.00-60.00	$70.00-80.00	$90.00-110.00
Spooner, 2³⁄₁₆"	$65.00-75.00	$70.00-80.00	$90.00-115.00
Sugar and Lid, 3¼"	$90.00-110.00	$100.00-130.00	$120.00-150.00
Table Set	$305.00-370.00	$400.00-465.00	$475.00-575.00

*Crystal with frosted panels, add 50%

Pointed Jewel "Long Diamond" No. 15006 (U.S. Glass Company)

	Crystal
Butter, 2"	$150.00-170.00
Creamer, 2⅞"	$60.00-70.00
Spooner, 2½"	$90.00-100.00
Sugar and Lid, 3⅞"	$100.00-125.00
Table Set	$400.00-465.00

Rex or Fancy Cut (Co-operative Flint Glass Co.)

According to trade catalogs, the official name of this pattern is "Rex." However many collectors continue to use the old term "Fancy Cut." Crystal pieces may be decorated with gold.

	Crystal		**Crystal**
*Butter, 2⅜"	$37.00-42.00	Tumbler, 1⅝"	$17.00-18.00
Creamer, 2½"	$25.00-27.00	Water Set	$152.00-168.00
Spooner, 2¾"	$27.00-30.00	Punch Bowl, 4⅜"	$100.00-125.00
Sugar and Lid, 4⅝"	$35.00-40.00	Punch Cup, 1¼"	$25.00-27.00
Table Set	$124.00-139.00	Punch Set, 7 pieces	$250.00-287.00
Pitcher, 3½"	$50.00-60.00		

*Teal, $150.00-175.00

"Rooster" No. 140 (King Glass Co.)

	Crystal
Butter, 2¾"	$175.00-200.00
Creamer, 3¼"	$110.00-130.00
Spooner, 3"	$150.00-175.00
Sugar and Lid, 5"	$170.00-190.00
Table Set	$605.00-695.00
Nappy, 3"	$120.00-140.00

Sandwich Ivy

	Crystal	**Amethyst**
Creamer, 2⅜"	$70.00-80.00	$110.00-125.00
Sugar, 3¼"	$70.00-80.00	$110.00-125.00

Sawtooth

	Crystal
Butter, 3"	$47.00-50.00
Creamer, 3½"	$30.00-32.00
Spooner, 3¼"	$37.00-40.00
Sugar and Lid, 4⅞"	$40.00-50.00
Table Set	$154.00-172.00

Sawtooth Band No. 1225 (A.H. Heisey and Co.)

Crystal sets may be found with gold trim or ruby flashing.

	***Crystal**	**Red Flashed**
Butter, 3⅞"	$150.00-160.00	$210.00-220.00
Creamer, 2½"	$50.00-60.00	$65.00-70.00
Spooner, 2¼"	$65.00-75.00	$70.00-80.00
Sugar and Lid, 4⅛"	$100.00-110.00	$140.00-150.00
Table Set	$365.00-405.00	$485.00-520.00

*With gold trim, add 10%

Sawtooth "Variation"

	Crystal
Butter, 4"	$65.00-70.00
Creamer, 3¾"	$30.00-32.00
Spooner, 3"	$35.00-37.00
Sugar and Lid, 5"	$50.00-55.00
Table Set	$180.00-194.00

Standing Lamb

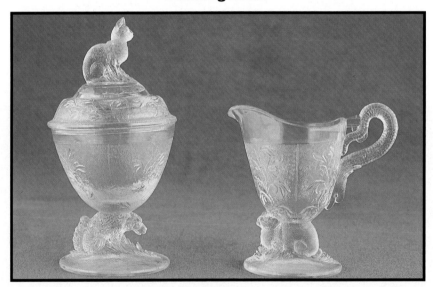

Standing Lamb is a four-piece table set which prominently features animal figures. Standing Lamb is a slightly confusing name since this figure is only used for the finial of the butter and does not appear on the other pieces to the set. The figure of a stork connects the bowl of the spooner to its base. The sugar and creamer both utilize two different animals. The handle of the creamer is formed from a snake and the body is resting on a rabbit which is lying comfortably on the foot. The body of the sugar is atop a seated dog and the figure of a seated cat proudly forms the finial of the lid. This is one of the more desirable sets in Pattern Glass. The entire set is scarce, but the spooner is probably most difficult to find.

	Crystal	Frosted
Butter	$850.00-900.00	$875.00-950.00
Creamer, 3¼"	$650.00-700.00	$675.00-725.00
Spooner	$950.00-1,000.00	$975.00-1,100.00
Sugar and Lid, 5⅛"	$700.00-750.00	$725.00-775.00
Table Set	$3,150.00-3,350.00	$3,250.00-3,550.00

Stippled Diamond

	Crystal	Blue Amber
Butter, 2¼"	$75.00-90.00	$145.00-160.00
Creamer, 2¼"	$60.00-70.00	$90.00-100.00
Spooner, 2⅛"	$65.00-75.00	$95.00-110.00
Sugar and Lid, 3⅛"	$75.00-85.00	$120.00-130.00
Table Set	$275.00-320.00	$450.00-500.00

Stippled Raindrop and Dewdrop

	Crystal	Amber Cobalt
Butter, 1¾"	$90.00-110.00	$130.00-145.00
Creamer, 2¼"	$55.00-60.00	$95.00-110.00
Spooner, 2⅛"	$55.00-60.00	$100.00-115.00
Sugar and Lid, 3"	$75.00-85.00	$115.00-125.00
Table Set	$275.00-315.00	$440.00-495.00

Stippled Vines and Beads

	Crystal	Teal Amber	Sapphire Blue
Butter, 2⅜"	$95.00-110.00	$125.00-140.00	$125.00-145.00
Creamer, 2⅜"	$60.00-65.00	$90.00-100.00	$95.00-120.00
Spooner, 2⅛"	$60.00-65.00	$90.00-100.00	$95.00-110.00
Sugar and Lid, 3⅛"	$75.00-85.00	$120.00-130.00	$125.00-140.00
Table Set	$290.00-325.00	$425.00-470.00	$440.00-515.00

Sultan (McKee Glass Co.)

Sultan may by found with either a plain or a stippled background. Although all Sultan pieces are difficult to find, the ones with the stippled backgrounds are the most elusive.

	*Crystal	Green/ Green Frosted	Chocolate
Butter, 3¾"	$105.00-115.00	$250.00-300.00	$625.00-675.00
Creamer, 2½"	$55.00-60.00	$100.00-120.00	$285.00-310.00
Spooner, 2½"	$70.00-80.00	$100.00-125.00	$300.00-350.00
Sugar and Lid, 4½"	$100.00-125.00	$125.00-150.00	$375.00-425.00
Table Set	$330.00-380.00	$575.00-695.00	$1,585.00-1,760.00

*Crystal frosted, add 10%

Sunbeam No. 15139 "Twin Snowshoes" (U.S. Glass Co.)

	Crystal
Butter, 2"	$120.00-140.00
Creamer, 2⅞"	$60.00-65.00
Spooner, 2⅛"	$90.00-110.00
Sugar and Lid, 3⅛"	$95.00-115.00
Table Set	$365.00-430.00

Sweetheart (Cambridge Glass Co.)

	Crystal
Butter, 2"	$18.00-20.00
Creamer, 2¼"	$10.00-12.00
Spooner, 2"	$15.00-17.00
Sugar and Lid, 3"	$17.00-20.00
Table Set	$60.00-69.00

Tappan
(McKee Glass Co.)

This table set was originally produced in crystal by McKee in the early 1900's. The covered butter, creamer, and covered sugar were later made in colors by Kemple in the 1950's to the mid-1960's. Special red and blue sets were produced in 1963 to commemorate the West Virginia centennial. Collectors are attracted to these later brightly colored sets and are adding them to their collections at reasonable prices.

	Crystal	Colors
*Butter, 3"	$29.00-34.00	$35.00-37.00
*Creamer, 2⅞"	$15.00-17.00	$22.00-25.00
Spooner, 2⅝"	$20.00-25.00	
*Sugar and Lid, 4"	$19.00-22.00	$27.00-30.00
Table Set	$83.00-98.00	$84.00-92.00

*Reproduced in white milk glass, amethyst, teal, green, red, blue, and amber.

Tulip and Honeycomb (Federal Glass Co.)

	Crystal		Crystal
Butter, 3⅝"	$37.00-42.00	Punch Set	$67.00-84.00
Creamer, 2⅝"	$20.00-22.00	Bowl, oval, open, 1¾"	$55.00-65.00
Spooner, 2½"	$20.00-25.00	Bowl, rnd., open, 1¾"	$60.00-70.00
Sugar and Lid, 3¾"	$30.00-35.00	Dish, low, covered, 2⅜"	$45.00-55.00
Table Set	$87.00-124.00	Casserole, oval, covered, 3¼"	$75.00-80.00
Punch Bowl, 4¼"	$25.00-30.00	Casserole, rnd., covered, 3¼"	$75.00-80.00
*Punch Cup, 1¼"	$7.00-9.00	Vegetable Set	$310.00-350.00

*Also comes in aqua.

Children's Dishes

Twist No. 137 (Albany Glass Co.)

	Crystal	Crystal Frosted	Blue Opalescent	White or Vaseline Opalescent
Butter, 3⅝"	$25.00-27.00	$60.00-70.00	$175.00-200.00	$135.00-145.00
Creamer, 2½"	$15.00-18.00	$50.00-55.00	$130.00-150.00	$85.00-95.00
Spooner, 2⅜"	$18.00-22.00	$40.00-50.00	$160.00-180.00	$95.00-110.00
Sugar and Lid, 3⅞"	$25.00-30.00	$60.00-80.00	$160.00-190.00	$120.00-140.00
Table Set	$83.00-97.00	$210.00-255.00	$625.00-720.00	$435.00-490.00

Two Band

	Crystal
Butter, 2"	$65.00-75.00
Creamer, 2¾"	$30.00-40.00
Spooner, 2⅞"	$45.00-50.00
Sugar and Lid, 3¾"	$55.00-65.00
Table Set	$195.00-230.00

Wee Branches

In addition to crystal, the mug may be found in white milk glass, blue milk glass, and transparent cobalt.

	Crystal		**Crystal**	**Blue/ Blue Milk Glass**
Butter, 1⅝"	$110.00-125.00	Cup, 1⅝"	$40.00-45.00	
Creamer, 2³⁄₁₆"	$65.00-75.00	Saucer, 3"	$12.00-15.00	
Spooner, 2½"	$75.00-85.00	Mug, 2"	$35.00-45.00	$50.00-60.00
Sugar and Lid, 2⅞"	$95.00-110.00	Plate, 3"	$50.00-60.00	
Table Set	$340.00-395.00			

Wheat Sheaf No. 500 (Cambridge Glass Company)

	Crystal
Master Berry, 2¼"	$35.00-45.00
Small Berry, 1"	$7.50-8.50
Berry Set, 7 pieces	$80.00-96.00
Wine Jug, 4⅛"	$60.00-70.00
Tumbler, 1¾"	$13.00-15.00
Wine Set, 7 pieces	$143.00-170.00

	Crystal	**White Milk Glass**
Punch Bowl, 3½"	$28.00-32.00	
Punch Cup, 1¼"	$7.50-8.50	$18.00-20.00
Punch Set, 7 pieces	$73.00-83.00	

Whirligig No. 15101 (U.S. Glass Co.)

The punch cup has been reproduced in numerous colors. The original punch bowl has not been reproduced. Instead, a taller footed punch bowl has been fashioned by using an old jelly compote mold.

	Crystal
Butter, 2½"	$23.00-27.00
Creamer, 2¼"	$14.00-16.00
Spooner, 2¼"	$17.00-20.00
Sugar and Lid, 3¼"	$20.00-22.00
Table Set	$74.00-85.00
Punch Bowl, 4¾"	$30.00-35.00
*Punch Cup, 1³⁄₁₆"	$6.00-7.00
Punch Set, 7 pieces	$66.00-77.00

*Reproduced

Wild Rose (Greentown)

The table set was made in white milk glass. The punch set will be found in white milk glass, crystal, and occasionally in blue milk glass. The candlestick is elusive and was only made in crystal.

	*White Milk Glass
Butter, 3½"	$65.00-75.00
Creamer, 1¾"	$55.00-60.00
Spooner, 1¾"	$50.00-60.00
Sugar, no Lid, 1¾"	$55.00-60.00
Table Set	$230.00-255.00

	White Milk Glass	Blue Milk Glass
Punch Bowl, 4⅛"	$75.00-85.00	$100.00-110.00
Punch Cup, 1³⁄₁₆"	$18.00-20.00	$24.00-26.00
Punch Set, 7 pieces	$185.00-205.00	$240.00-265.00

*Red, blue or gold trim, add 25%

Wild Rose (Greentown)

	Crystal
Punch Bowl, 4⅛"	$100.00-125.00
Punch Cup, 1³⁄₁₆"	$22.00-25.00
Punch Set, 7 pieces	$225.00-250.00
Candlestick, 4⅛"	$100.00-125.00

Cups and Saucers

Top Row: Cat and dog, amber $80.00-90.00; crystal $50.00-55.00; blue $85.00-95.00
Bottom Row: Lion, $70.00-80.00; Opal Lace $40.00-50.00

Mugs

Top Row: Banded Block, amber $35.00-40.00; Stippled Forget-Me-Not, crystal $50.00-60.00; Beaded Arrow, crystal $30.00-32.00; Cat-at-Play, amber $55.00-65.00; Cat-at-Play, crystal $35.00-40.00; Butterfly, crystal $40.00-45.00

Center Row: Wee Branches, blue $50.00-60.00; Drum 2", crystal $35.00-40.00; Sawtooth, amber $37.00-42.00; Sawtooth, blue $42.00-47.00; Grapevine with Ovals, crystal $25.00-30.00

Bottom Row: Short Panel, blue $22.00-27.00; Bead and Shield, blue milk glass $40.00-45.00; Bead and Dart, blue $25.00-30.00

Mugs

Top Row: Fighting Cats, crystal $50.00-55.00; Pups and Chicks, amber $55.00-65.00; Pups and Chicks, vaseline $65.00-70.00; Cupid and Venus, crystal $52.00-57.00; Hook, crystal $22.00-25.00

Center Row: Lighthouse, crystal $35.00-40.00; Thousand Eye, vaseline $60.00-65.00; Thousand Eye, amber $47.00-50.00; Doyle No. 500, crystal $30.00-35.00; Doyle No. 500, blue $40.00-50.00

Bottom Row: Begging Dog, crystal $50.00-55.00; Paneled, blue $35.00-40.00; Liberty Bell, crystal $100.00-125.00

Mugs

Top Row: Drum, 2½" crystal $29.00-32.00; School Children, crystal $47.00-50.00; Drum, 2³/₁₆" crystal $18.00-20.00; Ribbed Forget-Me-Not, crystal $35.00-40.00

Center Row: School Children, blue $75.00-85.00; School Children, blue milk glass $75.00-85.00

Bottom Row: *Heisey Child's Mug, crystal $450.00-500.00
*Reproduced in colors

Banana Stands

Left to Right:
Palm Leaf Fan $40.00-50.00;
Palm Leaf Fan $40.00-50.00;
Beautiful Lady $35.00-45.00;
Daisy and Star $40.00-45.00

Left to Right:
Unknown $35.00-45.00;
Fine Cut Star and Fan $40.00-45.00;
Little Ladders $40.00-45.00;
Unknown $35.00-45.00

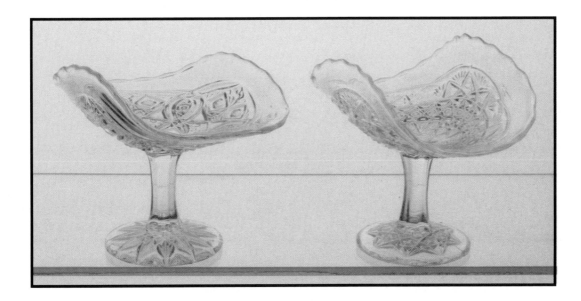

Left, 4¾" $35.00-40.00
Right, 5" $40.00-45.00

Cakestands

Front:
Rexford, 3¼"x6¼" $30.00-35.00
Rexford, 3½"x6¼" $30.00-35.00

Rear:
Ribbon Candy, 3⅜"x6⅜" $35.00-40.00
Ribbon Candy, 3⅜"x6⅜" $60.00-65.00
Unknown, 3⅜"x6¾" $35.00-45.00

Front:
Roses, 3⅜"x6⅜" $30.00-35.00
Peacock Feather, 2"x6¾" $85.00-95.00
Little Ladders, 3¼"x6⅛" $35.00-45.00

Rear:
Unknown, 4"x6¾" $35.00-45.00
Arrowhead & Oval, 3⅝"x6⅜"
    $35.00-45.00

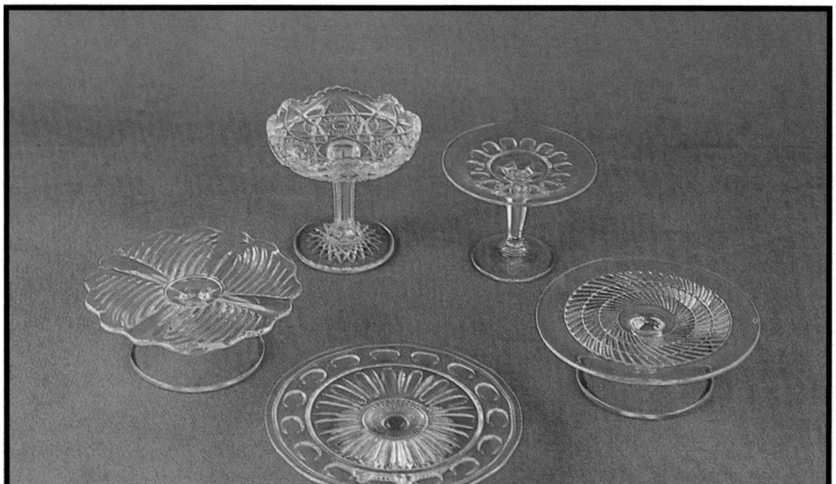

Front:
Thumbprint & Panels, 1"x6"
    $35.00-40.00

Center:
Swirl, 2"x5¼" $35.00-45.00
Inverted Swirl, 2"x5⅜" $35.00-40.00

Rear:
Twin Candy, 3⅜"x4" $35.00-45.00
Baby Thumbprint, 3"x4" $90.00-110.00

Cakestands

Front:
Candlewick small comport, 3⅛"x5⅝" $15.00-18.00

Center:
Buttons and Loops, 3⅝"x6⅜" $40.00-45.00
Unknown, 4"x6⅜" $32.00-37.00

Rear:
Beautiful Lady, 3½"x6" $35.00-40.00
Beautiful Lady, 3⅜"x6⅝" $35.00-40.00

Front:
Thumbprint Variation, 4¾" D $45.00-50.00
Flower with Band, 15" D $40.00-45.00

Rear:
Palm Leaf Fan, 5" D $40.00-45.00
Palm Leaf Fan, 6½" D $40.00-45.00
Palm Leaf Fan, 5¾" D $40.00-45.00

Candlesticks

Top Row:
> *Three-branch candles, all colors, 4⅜" $50.00-55.00

Center Row:
> **Swirl (French), amber, tall, 3⅝" $30.00-32.00
> White milk glass $18.00-20.00
> Green milk glass $40.00-45.00
> Blue milk glass $40.00-45.00
> Swirl Chamberstick (French), amber, short,1⅞" $25.00-30.00
> White milk glass $18.00-20.00
> Blue milk glass $30.00-35.00

Bottom Row:
> Fluted Chamberstick, cobalt, 2" $85.00-95.00
> ***Heisey, 2" $35.00-40.00
> Chamberstick, blue or green $35.00-40.00
> Banded Swirl, white, 2" $32.00-35.00
> Banded Swirl, crystal $15.00-20.00

*Three-branch candle reproduced in crystal, amberina, vaseline, Mother-of-Pearl, and cobalt.
**Swirl (French) reproduced in crystal.
***Heisey, 2" reproduced in crystal.

Candlesticks

Top Row:

Crystal, 4¼"	$35.00-40.00
Fine Rib, crystal, 4"	$45.00-50.00
Wild Rose, crystal, 4¼"	$100.00-125.00
Westmoreland, crystal, 4¼"	$40.00-42.00
Crystal, 4¾"	$40.00-42.00

Center Row:

Column, crystal, 4¾"	$50.00-55.00
Cobalt, 4"	$45.00-50.00
Peach, 4"	$35.00-40.00
Crystal, 4¼"	$40.00-45.00

Bottom Row:

Crystal (French), 2½"	$22.00-25.00
Cambridge, green, ⅝"	$22.00-25.00
Cambridge, blue, ⅝"	$22.00-25.00
Crystal, 2"	$27.00-30.00

Candlesticks

Top Row:

Three-branch, crystal, 4¼"	$50.00-60.00
Etched crystal, 4⅛"	$40.00-45.00
Lacy and Beads, cobalt, 2"	$80.00-90.00
Crystal, ⅝"	$15.00-18.00
Heisey, crystal, 4½"	$45.00-50.00

Center Row:

Crystal, 3¾"	$15.00-18.00
*Crystal, 3"	$22.00-25.00
Crystal, ⅝"	$15.00-18.00
Heisey, crystal, 3"	$40.00-45.00
**Heisey, crystal, 3½"	$37.00-42.00

Bottom Row:

***Dutch Boudoir, blue milk glass, 3"	$110.00-125.00
Westmoreland, crystal, 2½"	$22.00-25.00
Crystal, 2½"	$20.00-22.00
***Dutch Boudoir, white milk glass, 3"	$75.00-80.00

*Reproduced in crystal

**Heisey, 3½", reproduced in crystal and green

***Dutch Boudoir candlestick reproduced; new has "M" on base.

Candlesticks, Castor Sets, and Miniatures

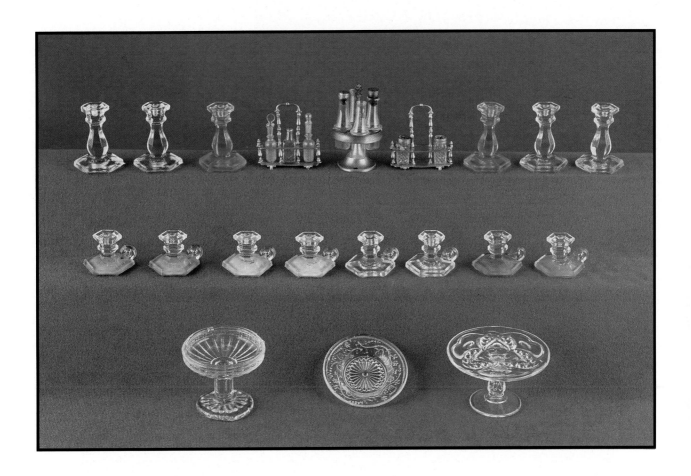

Top Row:

     Candles, 2⅛" yellow, green $125.00-135.00 pair

                   blue $150.00-155.00 pair

     Castor sets: Left, 2" $90.00-110.00

           Center, 2½" $110.00-125.00

           Right, 2" $65.00-75.00

Center Row:

     Candles, 1⅛" crystal $45.00-50.00 pair

     Cased, colored bases $90.00-100.00 pair

Bottom Row:

     Miniature Comport, 2½" $45.00-50.00

     Miniature Plate, 2½" $34.00-36.00

     Heart & Thumbprint Cakeplate, 1⅝" $145.00-155.00

Pewter Castor Sets

Top Row:

Banded Ring	$95.00-110.00
Shield	$110.00-120.00
Eagle in Circle	$130.00-140.00
Girl in Hoop	$140.00-150.00

Center Row:

Star (dated 1876)	$125.00-135.00
Resting Eagle	$115.00-130.00
Fancy Ring	$95.00-110.00

Bottom Row:

Fancy Wreath	$115.00-130.00
Angel in Ring	$115.00-130.00

Condiment Set

Left:
Hickman: Vinegar Cruet, 3"; Pepper, 3½";
Salt, 1"; Tray, 3¼" x 5"
Set: $95.00-110.00

Left Center:
Unknown, blue milk glass:
Pepper, 4¼"; Salt, 2½"; Tray, 3⅛" x 4¼"
Set: $80.00-90.00

Right Center:
Planet: Vinegar Cruet, 3"; Pepper 3¼";
Salt, 1"; Tray, 2½" x 6"
Set: $90.00-100.00

Right:
*English Hobnail: Vinegar Cruet, 2⅞";
Pepper, 3¼"; Salt, ⅞"; Tray, 5"
Set: colored $75.00-85.00
crystal $30.00-35.00

* Set reproduced in cobalt and crystal. Will probably also be made in other colors.

Decanter Set
(Bohemian)

The original decanter stopper is also red.
Decanter set, 5 pieces
$250.00-300.00

Decanter Set

This "Toy Liquor Set" has been authenticated in a 1910 Butler Brothers' catalogue.
If the set has gold trim, add 25% to the prices below.

Decanter, 8¼" $70.00-80.00   Tumbler, 1⅞" $8.00-9.00   Set, 5 pieces $120.00-130.00

Miscellaneous Miniatures

Top Row:
Swirl Creamer $50.00-55.00; Swirl Butter $55.00-60.00; Swirl Sugar and Lid $45.00-50.00; Swirl Creamer $40.00-50.00; Swirl Compote $45.00-50.00; Swirl Chamberpot $30.00-35.00; Swirl Chamberstick $12.00-14.00

Center Row:
Star Butterdish $65.00-70.00; Butterdish $30.00-35.00; Blue Butterdish $55.00-60.00; Butterdish $40.00-45.00; Covered Dish $30.00-35.00; Honey Dish $35.00-40.00; Covered Rectangular Dish $18.00-20.00

Bottom Row:
Buzz Saw Jug $35.00-40.00; D&M No. 42 Rose Bowl $67.00-75.00; Fenton Vases $35.00-45.00; Swirl Mug $4.00-6.00; Rose Bowl $70.00-80.00

Miniature Epergnes

Left: Epergne, 5" etched $125.00-135.00
Right: Epergne, 4¾" ruffled top $135.00-145.00

The Wedgewood-type pieces are marked "Made in Germany."

Miscellaneous

Syrup	$100.00-125.00
Planter, 2¾"	$80.00-95.00
Biscuit Jar, 3¾"	$100.00-125.00

Miniature Vases

These small vases were made by Sowerby's Elison Glass Works, Ltd., England. They have been found illustrated in an 1852 catalogue.

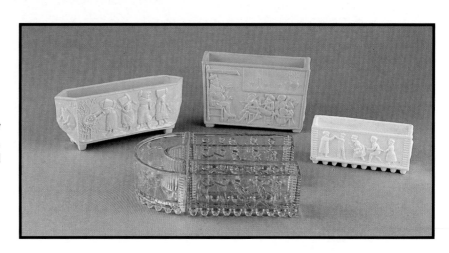

Front:
London Bridge, crystal rectangular, 1⅜" x 4½", $65.00-85.00; London Bridge, crystal, ½" round, 1⅜" x 4½", $70.00-90.00

Rear:
London Bridge, white milk glass, 1⅜" x 4½", $80.00-95.00; Old King Cole, blue milk glass, 1⅝" x 5", $100.00-125.00; Sunbonnet Babies, blue milk glass, hexagonal, 1⅜" x 6¼", $100.00-125.00

Spice Sets

Tall Spice, 6½"	$125.00-150.00
Medium Spice, 3½"	$80.00-100.00
Short Spice, 2"	$45.00-55.00

Ice Cream Maker

The Ice Cream freezer was first issued in 1932 by the White Mountain Freezer Company. It was reissued from original molds in 1989. Cost of the new issue was $44.95. Beware of any freezers with original paper labels. If the freezer is old the word "JUNIOR," in large letters, will occupy the entire center of the width of the diamond-shaped label. Above this will be "White Mountain" and below "Manufactured by the White Mountain Freezer Co., Nashua, N.H., U.S.A." If the freezer has no label, about the only way to ascertain age is to determine from the condition of the wood and metal whether the freezer is old or new.

Cone Holder	$90.00-125.00
Ice Tongs, 6"	$50.00-60.00
Ice Cream Freezer, 7½"	$175.00-225.00

Full-Size Children's Dishes

Alphabet Series (Hazel Atlas Co.)

Bowl, 5" $10.00-12.00   Mug, 2⅞" $8.00-10.00   Tumbler, $12.00-14.00

Animals (Hazel Atlas Co.)

Three Little Pigs		Scottie Dog	
Bowl, 7¾"	$12.00-15.00	Bowl, 5"	$20.00-25.00
Bowl, 5¾"	$12.00-15.00	Mug, 3"	$10.00-12.00
Mug, 3¾"	$10.00-12.00		
Mug, 3⅛"	$8.00-10.00		
Plate, 7"	$10.00-12.00	"Bosco" Mug, 3½"	$20.00-25.00

Circus Scenes (Hazel Atlas Co.)

Bowl, deep, 5"	$10.00-12.00	Plate, 8"	$8.00-10.00
Bowl, 5"	$10.00-12.00	Plate, divided	$10.00-12.00
Mug, 5¾"	$10.00-12.00	Plate, flashed	$8.00-10.00
Mug, flashed, 3¼"	$7.00-9.00	Tumbler, 5"	$3.00-4.00

Davy Crockett

Bowl (Fire King)	$8.00-10.00	Tumbler, 12 oz.	$14.00-16.00
Mug, 3¼" (Fire King)	$8.00-10.00	Tumbler, 10 oz.	$12.00-14.00
Mug (Hazel Atlas)	$18.00-20.00	Tumbler, 8 oz.	$12.00-14.00
Plate, 7"	$16.00-18.00		

Hopalong Cassidy (Hazel Atlas Co.)

Mug, 3"	$25.00-30.00	Tumbler, 10 oz. (red)	$35.00-40.00
Tumbler, 10 oz.	$27.00-30.00	Tumbler, 5 oz.	$60.00-65.00
Tumbler, 9 oz.	$35.00-40.00		

Hopalong Cassidy Mugs

Mug, left	$65.00-75.00
Mug, right	$65.00-75.00

Hopalong Cassidy and Other Cowboys

Bowl, 5"	$25.00-30.00	Mug, 3" (Indians)	$10.00-12.00
Mug, 3" (Tex)	$10.00-12.00	Plate, 7"	$25.00-27.00
Mug, 2¼" (Lone Ranger)	$30.00-35.00		

Cowboy Collectibles (Hazel Atlas Co.)

Bowl, 5" (Cisco Kid)	$18.00-22.00	Mug, 3" (Ranger Joe)	$9.00-11.00
Bowl, 5" (Ranger Joe)	$9.00-11.00	Mug, 3" (Wyatt Earp)	$22.00-27.00
Bowl, 5" (Wyatt Earp)	$25.00-30.00	Plate, 7"	$12.00-14.00
Bowl, 6⅝" divided	$8.00-10.00		

Depression Era Glass Tumblers

The ruby tumbler was made by the Hocking Glass Company and the two cobalt tumblers were made by the Hazel Atlas Glass Company.

Ruby "Howdy Wrangler"	$25.00-27.00
Cobalt "Tom Tom the Piper's Son"	$25.00-30.00
Cobalt "Mother Goose"	$30.00-35.00

Tumblers (Hazel Atlas Co.)

Top Row:
Mary Had a Little Lamb $15.00-18.00; Little Boy Blue $16.00-18.00; Butcher, Baker, and Candlestick Maker $16.00-18.00
Center Row:
Little Red Riding Hood $15.00-20.00; Mary Had a Little Lamb $16.00-18.00
Bottom Row:
Circus Clowns $11.00-13.00; The Old Lady in the Shoe $16.00-18.00; Jack and Jill $15.00-19.00

Miscellaneous Bowls and Mugs

The plate and the mug on the top right were made by Anchor Hocking. The bowl in the center right is marked "Fire King." The remainder of the pieces were made by Hazel Atlas.

Bowl, (Child's Prayer)	$6.00-9.00	Mug, 3" (Child's Prayer)	$6.00-9.00
Bowl, 7" (Bo Peep)	$18.00-20.00	Mug, 3⅛" (Bo Peep)	$12.00-14.00
Bowl, 5" (Gulliver)	$20.00-22.00	Mug, 3" (Robin Hood)	$25.00-30.00

Space Scenes (Hazel Atlas Co.)

Mug, 3" (Top Row)	$15.00-17.00
Mug, 3⅛" (Bottom Row)	$14.00-16.00

Shirley Temple

*Bowl, 6½"	$60.00-70.00
*Creamer, 4½"	$27.00-32.00
*Mug, 3¾"	$55.00-65.00

*Reproduced. Look for the new decal to be stark white and very granular in appearance. A juice tumbler is also currently being made by the Libbey Glass Company.

Shirley Temple Sugar $150.00-200.00

Depression Era Cereal Bowls

"Kelloggs" pink $80.00-90.00
"Bucking Horse," green $30.00-35.00

"Three Bears" Baby Bottles

"Three Bears" Bottle, 6¼" $9.00-11.00
Boxed Set $40.00-45.00

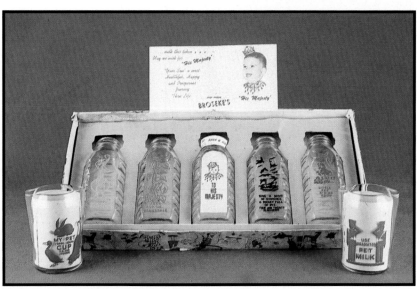

Baby Bottles

Baby Bottle $8.00-10.00
Boxed Set $40.00-50.00
"Pet" Measure $20.00-25.00

Baby Gift Set

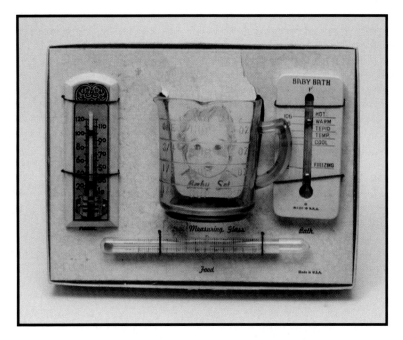

The ideal gift set for a newborn baby incorporated a transparent green one cup measure in a box with three useful thermometers. The thermometers gauged the temperature of the infant's food, bath water, and room.

Boxed Baby Set $125.00-150.00

Baby Reamers

Top Row:
White Milk Glass with Rabbit $95.00-110.00; Crystal $45.00-50.00
Center Row:
Green $100.00-125.00; Crystal Frosted with Chicks $60.00-80.00; Blue $150.00-175.00
Bottom Row:
Pink $100.00-145.00; Crystal $65.00-70.00; Green $100.00-150.00

Baby Reamers

Top Row:
Green $175.00-200.00; Pink $150.00-180.00; Amber $175.00-200.00
Center Row:
Crystal (left) $40.00-45.00; Crystal (right) $40.00-45.00
Bottom Row:
Crystal Frosted $75.00-85.00

Baby Reamers

This white milk glass reamer decorated with a
white enameled bear holding colored balloons was
made by the Fenton Glass Company.

Enameled Reamer $185.00-200.00

PART 2: CHINA AND POTTERY
European

Fish Set (Austria)

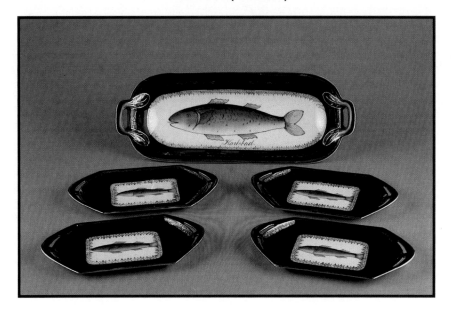

Plate, 6½"	$25.00-30.00
Platter, 11¼"	$75.00-95.00
Set, 7 pieces	$225.00-275.00

Silhouette Children (Victoria/Czechoslovakia)

Creamer, 2⅛"	$10.00-12.00
Cup, 1⅞"	$5.00-8.00
Plate	$5.00-6.00
Saucer, 3¼"	$1.00-1.50
Sugar and Lid	$14.00-16.00
Teapot and Lid, 3⅝"	$27.00-32.00
Set, 4 places	$100.00-125.00

English Dinner Sets

"Kite Fliers" (England)

This English dinnerware service dates to the early 1800's and is called "Kite Fliers" by many collectors. The transfer design is from a print titled "Old Age and Careless Youth" by English print maker Thomas Bewick. The design features a man in Colonial dress watching a boy fly a kite. Another boy to their right is rolling a hoop.

Gravy Boat, 3¼"	$95.00-100.00	Tureen, 2½" x 3¼"	$125.00-150.00
Plate, 2½"	$42.00-46.00	Tureen, 3¼" x 4¼"	$125.00-150.00
Plate, 2¾"	$44.00-48.00	Underplate, 3½" x 5¼"	$90.00-95.00
Plate, 3½"	$44.00-48.00	Vegetable, covered, 3½"	$100.00-110.00
Soup Bowl, 3½"	$50.00-55.00		

"Fancy Loop"

Bowl, oval, 4½"	$22.00-25.00	Platter, 6"	$22.00-26.00
Gravy Boat, 2"	$25.00-30.00	Platter, rnd. 2-H, 4½"	$22.00-25.00
Plate, 3"	$5.00-6.00	Platter, rnd. 2-H, 5½"	$22.00-25.00
Plate, 3¼"	$5.50-6.50	Soup Bowl, 3¾"	$10.00-12.00
Platter, 4½"	$18.00-20.00	Vegetable, covered, 2½"	$35.00-45.00
Platter, 5"	$20.00-22.00		

Myrtle Wreath (J.M. & S.)

Bowl, oval, 5"	$25.00-27.00	Platter, 6½"	$25.00-30.00
Gravy Boat, 2¾"	$27.00-30.00	Tray, 2-H, 4¾"	$20.00-25.00
Plate, 3¼"	$5.00-6.00	Tureen, 3½"	$45.00-65.00
Plate, 3¾"	$5.00-6.00	Tureen, 4½"	$50.00-70.00
Platter, 4"	$20.00-22.00	Vegetable, covered, 4¾"	$45.00-65.00
Platter, 5¾"	$22.00-25.00		

Athens

This dinner set was produced by Davenport in the mid-1800's.

Gravy Boat, 1¾"	$30.00-32.00	Tureen, 3½"	$40.00-45.00
Plate, 3"	$5.00-8.00	Tureen, 4¼"	$45.00-50.00
Plate, 3¼"	$6.00-9.00	Tureen Underplate, 4¼"	$10.00-12.00
Plate, 3¾"	$6.00-9.00	Tureen Underplate, 5½"	$12.00-14.00
Platter, 4½"	$20.00-25.00	Vegetable, covered, 2¾"	$60.00-75.00
Platter, 5½"	$25.00-27.00		

Blue Marble (England)

Bowl, oval, 4½"	$35.00-45.00	Tureen, 4¼"	$55.00-70.00
Gravy Boat, 1½"	$45.00-55.00	Tureen, 3½"	$65.00-75.00
Plate, 4"	$12.00-15.00	Underplate, 5½"	$32.00-35.00
Platter, 4½"	$35.00-45.00	Underplate, 4½"	$30.00-32.00

Dimity

Soup Bowl, 4¼"	$8.00-10.00	Tray, round, 4½"	$15.00-18.00
Plate, 3½"	$4.00-5.00	Tray, round, 5¼"	$18.00-20.00
Tray, rect., 4⅞"	$15.00-18.00	Vegetable, covered, 2¼"	$30.00-35.00
Tray, rect., 5¾"	$15.00-18.00		

Blue Banded Ironstone

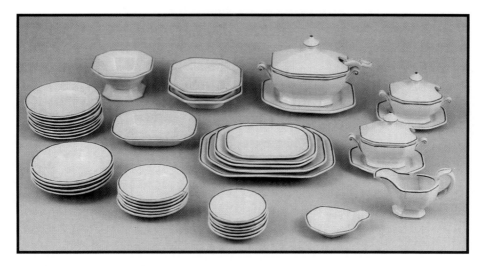

The backstamp of this large English dinnerware set is simply "Iron Stone."
The blank is the same as other dinner sets produced by Minton.

Bowl, 8-sided, 4"	$18.00-20.00	Platter, 5⅛"	$18.00-20.00
Bowl, oval, 4⅜"	$25.00-27.00	Platter, 6"	$20.00-25.00
Compote, 3¼"	$30.00-35.00	Platter, 6¾"	$22.00-26.00
Gravy Boat, 2⅛"	$25.00-27.00	Server, 1-H, 3"	$8.00-10.00
Plate, 2⅝"	$4.00-5.00	Soup Bowl, 4"	$8.00-10.00
Plate, 3¼"	$5.00-6.00	Tureen, 4½" x 5½"	$35.00-55.00
Plate, 4"	$5.00-6.00	Tureen Underplate, 3¾" x 5"	$8.00-12.00
Platter, 4¼"	$15.00-18.00		

Minton "Flow Blue Dogwood"

Bowl, oval, 4⅜"	$40.00-50.00	Platter, 5"	$40.00-50.00
Soup Bowl, 4⅛"	$30.00-40.00	Platter, 6"	$37.00-40.00
Casserole, 4½"	$75.00-95.00	Platter, 6¾"	$45.00-50.00
Gravy Boat, 2⅛"	$50.00-65.00	Server, 1-H, 3"	$25.00-30.00
Plate, 2⅝"	$12.00-14.00	Tureen, 4½"	$75.00-85.00
Plate, 3¼"	$15.00-18.00	Tureen, 6½"	$100.00-110.00
Plate, 4"	$18.00-22.00	Vegetable, covered, 3"	$90.00-100.00

Forget-Me-Not

This is an unusual "Flow Blue" type English dinnerware set with exceptional quality. The large number of pieces available enhances the desirability of the set. The blue which is flowing into the white background adds to the attractiveness of the set. The name Forget-Me-Not is from *Children's Glass Dishes, China and Furniture,* Vol. II by Lechler.

Bowl, oval, 4¾"	$65.00-90.00	Platter, 6½"	$85.00-95.00
Casserole, 4¾"	$125.00-145.00	Server, 1-H, 2¾"	$35.00-40.00
Gravy Boat, 2"	$90.00-100.00	Soup Bowl, 3¾"	$35.00-45.00
Plate, 2¾"	$18.00-20.00	Tureen, 3⅞"	$95.00-125.00
Plate, 3⅛"	$20.00-25.00	Tureen, 5"	$125.00-145.00
Plate, 3¾"	$25.00-35.00	Tureen Underplate, 4"	$25.00-35.00
Platter, 4¾"	$55.00-80.00	Tureen Underplate, 5"	$35.00-40.00
Platter, 5½"	$70.00-85.00		

Fishers ("C.E. & M.")

The English mark, "C.E. & M." stands for the Staffordshire pottery of Cork, Edge, and Malkin. The color of this set is dark green, but other colors including blue and purple may be found.

Bowl, oval, 3"	$18.00-22.00	Platter, 5"	$27.00-30.00
Gravy Boat, 3"	$25.00-27.00	Soup Bowl, 4"	$12.00-14.00
Plate, 2¼"	$5.00-6.00	Tureen, 3½"	$45.00-50.00
Plate, 3¼"	$5.00-6.00	Tureen Underplate, 5"	$12.00-15.00
Plate, 4"	$6.00-7.00	Vegetable, covered, 5½"	$45.00-50.00
Platter, 3¾"	$25.00-27.00		

"Twin Flower" Flow Blue

Bowl, oval, 4¾"	$60.00-80.00	Gravy boat, 2½"	$65.00-85.00
Bowl, oval, 5"	$65.00-85.00	Plate, 3¾"	$18.00-20.00
Bowl, deep oval, 3¾"	$75.00-100.00	Platter, 4½"	$60.00-80.00
Casserole, 4"	$80.00-95.00	Platter, 5½"	$70.00-90.00
Casserole, 5"	$85.00-110.00	Soup Bowl	$35.00-45.00

Scenes From England

The DeGout Castle is featured on the plate and the soup bowl in this set. The vegetable bowl pictures Leclad's Bridge. These pieces are part of a dinner set in which each piece depicts an English scene. Some of the scenes on other pieces which are not shown are Tewkesbury Church, Sysham Monastery, Lonington Park, Blaize Castle, and Kenilworth Park.

Plate, 3⅛"	$30.00-35.00
Soup Bowl, 3⅝"	$40.00-50.00
Vegetable, covered, 3⅞"	$100.00-145.00

Roman Chariots (Cauldon, England)

Creamer, 2"	$32.00-37.00	Sugar, 1½"	$35.00-40.00
Cup, 1¾"	$27.00-30.00	Teapot and Lid, 3⅜"	$95.00-110.00
Saucer	$6.00-8.00	Set, 6 Places	$360.00-420.00

Acorn (Cork, Edge and Malkin, Burlsem)

Creamer, 2⅛"	$16.00-18.00	Sugar and Lid, 3½"	$22.00-25.00
Cup, 2"	$10.00-12.00	Teapot and Lid, 3½"	$45.00-55.00
Plate, 4⅞"	$5.00-6.00	Waste Bowl, 4⅜"	$25.00-30.00
Saucer, 4¾"	$2.00-3.00	Set, 6 Places	$210.00-255.00

Gaudy Ironstone (England)

Creamer, 2⅜"	$35.00-40.00	Sugar and Lid, 4"	$50.00-60.00
Cup, 1⅞"	$32.00-35.00	Teapot and Lid, 4½"	$140.00-160.00
Plate, 6"	$35.00-45.00	Waste Bowl, 2⅞"	$75.00-95.00
Saucer	$12.00-15.00	Set, 6 Places	$590.00-700.00

Amherst Japan (England)

Amherst Japan is a very gaudy oriental design emphasizing interesting combinations of blue and orange. This set was produced by Minton during the mid-1800's.

Creamer, 2½"	$35.00-38.00	Sugar and Lid, 2½"	$45.00-55.00
Cup, 1¾"	$30.00-32.00	Teapot and Lid, 4¼"	$140.00-160.00
Plate, 5"	$15.00-18.00	Waste Bowl, 4½"	$75.00-85.00
Saucer, 4½"	$10.00-12.00	Set, 6 Places	$625.00-710.00

By the Mill

This brown transfer mill scene tea set was produced by David Methvin & Sons of Scotland. Three people are featured in the foreground while the background is comprised of an old mill. This set will also be found in red or blue.

Creamer	$25.00-27.00	Sugar and Lid	$30.00-32.00
Cup	$15.00-18.00	Teapot and Lid	$50.00-60.00
Plate	$8.00-10.00	Waste Bowl	$30.00-35.00
Saucer	$3.00-4.00	Set, 6 Places	$290.00-345.00

Copeland's Blue Animal Set

This English tea set was made by W.T. Copeland and Sons, Spode Works, Stoke-On-Trent, during the early 1900's. A complete set consists of a teapot and lid, a covered sugar, creamer, waste bowl, six cups and saucers, six plates, and two square serving dishes.

Creamer	$18.00-20.00	Sugar and Lid	$22.00-25.00
Cup	$14.00-16.00	Teapot and Lid, 4"	$75.00-85.00
Plate, 3¾"	$6.00-8.00	Waste Bowl	$30.00-40.00
Plate, 2-H 5"	$20.00-25.00	Set, 6 Places	$245.00-320.00
Saucer, 4½"	$2.00-3.00		

"Butterfly" Tea Set

Creamer, 3¼"	$8.00-10.00	Sugar and Lid, 3½"	$12.00-14.00
Cup, 2"	$5.00-8.00	Teapot and Lid, 4¼"	$45.00-50.00
Plate, 5"	$5.00-6.00	Waste Bowl, 4"	$27.00-30.00
Platter, 2-H, 6¼"	$12.00-14.00	Set, 6 Places	$200.00-225.00
Saucer, 4¼"	$2.00-3.00		

Mini Floral Tea Set

Creamer, 3½"	$9.00-12.00	Sugar and Lid, 3¾"	$14.00-16.00
Cup, 2⅛"	$8.00-10.00	Teapot and Lid, 6½"	$45.00-50.00
Plate, 5"	$6.00-8.00	Tray, 7"	$16.00-18.00
Saucer, 4⅜"	$2.00-3.00	Set, 6 Places	$190.00-225.00

Blue Onion Tea Set

Cup	$18.00-20.00	Sugar and Lid	$27.00-32.00
Creamer	$22.00-27.00	Teapot and Lid	$60.00-70.00
Plate	$8.00-10.00	Set, 6 Places	$290.00-340.00
Saucer	$4.00-5.00		

Tan Luster and White Tea Set

Creamer, 3¼"	$10.00-12.00	Sugar and Lid, 3½"	$12.00-14.00
Cup, 1¾"	$10.00-12.00	Teapot and Lid, 5¼"	$45.00-50.00
Plate, 3¼"	$4.00-5.00	Set, 6 Places	$165.00-195.00
Saucer, 3"	$2.00-2.50		

Children's Dishes

Pink Banded Floral Tea Set

Creamer, 3½"	$10.00-12.00	Sugar and Lid, 4½"	$14.00-16.00
Cup, 2¼"	$5.00-6.00	Teapot and Lid, 5½"	$30.00-40.00
Saucer, 4¾"	$1.50-2.00	Set, 6 Places	$90.00-115.00

Mary Had a Little Lamb (Brentleigh Ware Staffordshire, England)

Creamer, 1½"	$10.00-12.00	Sugar, open, 1⅛"	$10.00-12.00
Cup, 1⅞"	$8.00-10.00	Teapot and Lid, 3½"	$45.00-55.00
Plate, 3¾"	$6.00-8.00	Set, 6 Places	$160.00-200.00
Saucer, 3⅜"	$1.50-2.00		

Pink Luster Sets (Germany)

	Hunt Scene	Chauffeur with Lady
Creamer	$22.00-27.00	$22.00-27.00
Cup	$18.00-20.00	$18.00-20.00
Plate	$10.00-12.00	$10.00-12.00
Saucer	$4.00-5.00	$4.00-5.00
Sugar and Lid	$30.00-32.00	$30.00-32.00
Teapot and Lid	$85.00-95.00	$95.00-110.00
Set, 6 Place	$330.00-380.00	$340.00-395.00

Children Luster Sets

	Children's Scenes	Children with Teddy Bear
Creamer, 2½"	$18.00-22.00	$27.00-30.00
Cup, 1⅞"	$14.00-16.00	$20.00-25.00
Plate, 5¼"	$8.00-10.00	$12.00-14.00
Saucer, 8⅛"	$4.00-5.00	$4.00-5.00
Sugar and Lid, 3½"	$22.00-27.00	$30.00-35.00
Teapot and Lid, 5¼"	$100.00-125.00	
Teapot and Lid, (Teddy Bear) 4½"		$100.00-125.00
Set, 6 Places	$235.00-310.00	$375.00-435.00

Teddy Bear Tea Set

Creamer	$28.00-35.00	Sugar and Lid, 4"	$37.00-42.00
Cup, 2"	$25.00-30.00	Teapot and Lid, 6½"	$120.00-150.00
Plate, 5"	$12.00-15.00	Set, 6 Places	$432.00-525.00
Saucer, 4¼"	$4.00-5.00		

"Friends" Tea Set (Germany)

Creamer, 2⅝"	$22.00-27.00	Sugar and Lid, 3⅝"	$30.00-32.00
Cup, 1⅞"	$16.00-18.00	Teapot and Lid, 5½"	$75.00-90.00
Plate	$8.00-10.00	Set, 6 Places	$295.00-345.00
Saucer, 4¼"	$4.00-5.00		

"Dutch Windmill" Tea Set

Notice this decal will be found on sets utilizing different blanks. The teapot, waste bowl, and cup and saucer on the left are from one set and the sugar, creamer, and three cups in the front are part of another set.

Creamer, 3½"	$16.00-19.00	Sugar and Lid	$22.00-25.00
Cup, 2¼"	$12.00-14.00	Teapot and Lid, 6½"	$70.00-80.00
Plate	$6.00-8.00	Waste Bowl, 2¼"	$25.00-45.00
Saucer, 4⅝"	$4.00-5.00	Set, 6 Places	$260.00-315.00

"Playful Cats" Tea Set

Creamer, 3¼"	$25.00-27.00	Sugar and Lid, 2¾"	$27.00-32.00
Cup, 2⅛"	$20.00-25.00	Teapot and Lid, 5¼"	$130.00-150.00
Plate, 5¼"	$12.00-14.00	Set, 6 Places	$395.00-460.00
Saucer, 4¼"	$4.00-5.00		

Blue Portrait Tea Set (Germany)

Creamer, 2¾"	$25.00-27.00	Sugar and Lid, 2⅞"	$28.00-32.00
Cup, 1⅝"	$18.00-20.00	Teapot and Lid, 4½"	$70.00-75.00
Plate, 3½"	$8.00-10.00	Tray, 5"	$22.00-25.00
Saucer, 3¼"	$4.00-4.50	Set, 4 Places	$265.00-300.00

"Brundage Girls" (Germany)

Creamer, 4"	$27.00-32.00	Plate, 6¼"	$20.00-25.00
Cup, 1³⁄₁₆"	$18.00-20.00	Saucer, 4"	$4.00-5.00
Mug, 2¾"	$30.00-35.00		

"The Bridesmaid" (Germany)

Creamer, 3⅜"	$20.00-22.00	Sugar and Lid, 3"	$25.00-27.00
Cup, 2½"	$20.00-22.00	Teapot and Lid, 4½"	$80.00-90.00
Plate, 6½"	$8.00-10.00	Set, 6 Places	$320.00-360.00
Saucer, 4⅞"	$4.00-5.00	Mug, 2⅝"	$70.00-90.00

"Children With Toy Animals" Tea Set

Creamer, 3¼"	$16.00-18.00	Sugar	$16.00-18.00
Cup, 2"	$10.00-12.00	Teapot and Lid, 4¼"	$55.00-65.00
Plate	$5.00-8.00	Set, 6 Places	$215.00-270.00
Saucer, 4¼"	$3.00-4.00		

Happifats (Rudolstadt, Made in Germany)

Happifats is a German coffee set featuring decals with very active children. Two variations depict children with blue-trimmed pieces among strawberries, or with yellow-trimmed pieces and the children frolicking among raspberries. These sets first appeared in 1914 and were popular through the twenties.

Coffee Pot, 5¾"	$100.00-125.00	Saucer, 4½"	$4.00-5.00
Cup, 2"	$20.00-22.00	Sugar and Lid, 2½"	$25.00-30.00
Creamer, 3"	$20.00-25.00	Set, 6 Places	$350.00-415.00
Plate, 5¼"	$10.00-12.00		

Kewpies Tea Set

The teapot is marked "Copyrighted Mrs. Rose O' Neill Wilson – Kewpies – Bavaria."
Some sets will also be found with dinner plates.

Creamer	$40.00-45.00	Sugar and Lid	$50.00-60.00
Cup	$40.00-50.00	Teapot and Lid	$200.00-250.00
Saucer	$10.00-15.00	Set, 6 Places	$590.00-745.00

"Buster Brown" (Germany)

Creamer, 2⅞"	$30.00-35.00	Sugar and Lid, 3¾"	$60.00-70.00
Cup, 2½"	$30.00-35.00	Teapot and Lid, 5⅞"	$145.00-165.00
Plate, 5"	$28.00-30.00	Set, 6 Places	$500.00-600.00
Saucer, 4⅝"	$4.00-5.00		

"The House That Jack Built" (Germany)

Creamer, 3⅜"	$15.00-18.00	Sugar and Lid, 3½"	$20.00-22.00
Cup, 1⅞"	$12.00-14.00	Teapot and Lid, 5¾"	$70.00-80.00
Plate, 5¼"	$6.00-8.00	Set, 6 Places	$225.00-260.00
Saucer, 4"	$3.00-4.00		

Nursery Rhyme Set (Germany)

Creamer, 1⅞"	$12.00-15.00	Sugar, 1⅜"	$12.00-15.00
Cup, 1¾"	$8.00-10.00	Teapot and Lid	$40.00-50.00
Plate	$4.00-6.00	Set, 6 Places	$155.00-200.00
Saucer, 3¾"	$3.00-4.00		

Nursery Scenes (Germany)

Creamer, 3"	$11.00-13.00	Sugar and Lid, 3¼"	$18.00-20.00
Cup, 2"	$7.00-8.00	Teapot and Lid, 4½"	$45.00-55.00
Plate	$4.00-4.50	Set, 6 Places	$145.00-175.00
Saucer	$2.00-3.00		

Green Luster "Standing Pony" Tea Set

Creamer, 3¼"	$12.00-14.00	Sugar and Lid	$15.00-20.00
Cup, 2"	$14.00-16.00	Teapot and Lid, 6"	$60.00-65.00
Plate	$6.00-8.00	Set, 6 Places	$200.00-275.00
Saucer, 4¼"	$4.00-5.00		

"Barnyard Animals" Tea Set

Creamer, 3⅜"	$10.00-12.00	Sugar and Lid, 4"	$15.00-18.00
Cup, 2⅛"	$10.00-14.00	Teapot and Lid, 5¾"	$55.00-60.00
Plate, 5½"	$6.00-8.00	Set, 6 Places	$210.00-230.00
Saucer, 4½"	$4.00-5.00		

"Pink Rose" Tea Set

Creamer, 3¼"	$9.00-11.00	Sugar and Lid, 4"	$12.00-15.00
Cup, 2¼"	$8.00-10.00	Teapot and Lid, 6¼"	$45.00-52.00
Plate, 5⅛"	$5.00-5.50	Set, 6 Places	$160.00-185.00
Saucer, 4¼"	$2.00-3.00		

"Red and White Rose" Tea Set

Creamer, 3¼"	$10.00-12.00	Sugar and Lid, 3¾"	$14.00-16.00
Cup, 2¼"	$9.00-10.00	Teapot and Lid, 6"	$55.00-65.00
Plate, 5"	$6.00-7.00	Set, 6 Places	$185.00-215.00
Saucer, 4½"	$3.00-4.00		

Floral Set (Germany)

Creamer	$12.00-14.00	Sugar and Lid, 3½"	$15.00-18.00
Cup, 2³⁄₁₆"	$9.00-11.00	Teapot and Lid, 5¼"	$55.00-65.00
Plate	$5.00-6.00	Set, 6 Places	$185.00-220.00
Saucer, 4⅜"	$3.50-4.50		

Blue Heart Border with Orange Flower Tea Set (G. B. H. Co. Bavaria)

Creamer, 2¾"	$8.00-10.00	Sugar and Lid, 3½"	$12.00-14.00
Cup, 2¼"	$5.00-8.00	Teapot and Lid, 4¼"	$25.00-30.00
Plate, 5¾"	$4.00-5.00	Set, 6 Places	$115.00-150.00
Saucer, 4½"	$2.00-3.00		

Viktoria Pink Floral Tea Set (Effenbein, Rosenthal, Kronach-Germany)

Creamer, 2¾"	$12.00-14.00	Sugar and Lid, 3½"	$15.00-18.00
Cup, 1½"	$8.00-10.00	Teapot and Lid, 7"	$55.00-65.00
Plate, 6"	$5.00-8.00	Set, 6 Places	$180.00-220.00
Saucer, 4¾"	$3.00-4.00		

ABC Animal Tea Set

Creamer, 2⅝"	$12.00-14.00	Sugar and Lid, 4¼"	$16.00-18.00
Cup, 2"	$10.00-12.00	Teapot and Lid, 5¼"	$55.00-60.00
Plate, 5¼"	$5.00-8.00	Set, 6 Places	$200.00-245.00
Saucer, 4"	$4.00-5.00		

Coffee Set (Germany)

Coffee Pot, 6"	$35.00-45.00	Saucer, 4"	$2.00-3.00
Creamer, 2⅜"	$8.00-10.00	Sugar and Lid, 3¾"	$10.00-14.00
Cup, 2⅛"	$5.00-8.00	Set, 4 Places	$100.00-120.00
Plate, 5¼"	$4.00-5.00		

Floral Tea Sets (Germany)

	Pink	**Blue**
Creamer	$6.00-8.00	$6.00-8.00
Cup	$4.00-6.00	$5.00-7.00
Plate	$3.00-4.00	$4.00-5.00
Saucer	$1.00-2.00	$1.50-2.50
Sugar and Lid	$8.00-10.00	$12.00-14.00
Teapot and Lid	$25.00-30.00	$25.00-30.00
Set, 6 Places	$85.00-115.00	$105.00-135.00

Floral Tea Set (Germany)

Creamer	$10.00-12.00	Sugar and Lid	$14.00-16.00
Cup	$8.00-10.00	Teapot and Lid	$30.00-35.00
Plate	$5.00-7.00	Set, 6 Places	$147.00-185.00
Saucer	$2.00-3.00		

Floral and Gold Cabaret Set

Creamer, 3¼"; Cup, 1¾"; Saucer, 3¾"; Sugar and Lid, 3"; Teapot and Lid, 3"; Tray, 8¾"
Set, 2 Places $400.00-500.00

Floral Cabaret Set (Dresden)

Creamer, 2½"; Cup, 2⅛"; Saucer, 4"; Sugar and Lid, 3"; Teapot and Lid, 4¾"; Tray, 8¼" x 9⅝"
Set, 2 Places $250.00-325.00

Cabaret Sets (Germany)

Set, 2 Places

White/Blue	$125.00-175.00
Pink/Gold	185.00-225.00

Karlsbad Dinner Set

Bowl, round, 3½"	$8.00-10.00	Gravy Boat, 3¼"	$10.00-12.00
Bowl, square, 2¾"	$8.00-10.00	Plate, 3½"	$4.00-5.00
Casserole, 5"	$10.00-12.00	Plate, 4⅛"	$3.00-4.00

Stein Set (Bavaria)

Stein (Character), 1⅞"	$15.00-18.00
Stein (Shield), 1⅞"	$8.00-10.00
Tray, 5¾" x 7⅞"	$25.00-27.00

Blue Onion Kitchenware (Germany)

Box, Mehl, 4¼"	$200.00-225.00	Meat Tenderizer, 7"	$160.00-180.00
Salt Box, 4¼"	$200.00-225.00	Rolling Pin, 8"	$275.00-325.00
Egg Whip, 4½"	$125.00-150.00	Spoon, 5½"	$130.00-135.00

Figural Spice Set (Germany)

Canister, 2½"	$35.00-40.00
Canister, 3¾"	$45.00-50.00
Oil, Vinegar, 3½"	$45.00-65.00
Salt Box, 3¼"	$75.00-100.00
Set, 15 Pieces	$650.00-770.00

Blue Banded Spice Set (Germany)

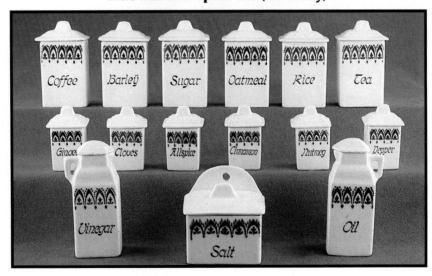

Canister, 2½"	$20.00-25.00	Salt Box, 3⅛"	$40.00-50.00
Canister, 3⅝"	$25.00-28.00	Set, 15 Pieces	$360.00-400.00
Oil, Vinegar, 4¼"	$25.00-35.00		

Floral Spice Set (Germany)

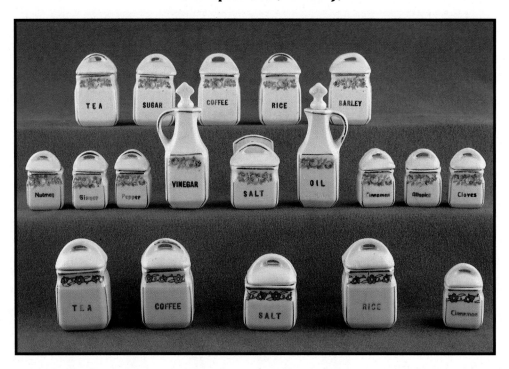

Although the canisters in the bottom row are the same size and shape as those pictured above them, their floral design is slightly different. They are part of a different set, but are so similar that they have been priced together.

Canister, 2⅛"	$18.00-25.00	Salt Box, 1⅞"	$30.00-35.00
Canister, 1¾"	$15.00-22.00	Set, 15 Pieces	$250.00-340.00
Oil, Vinegar, 3⅜"	$25.00-27.00		

Spice Sets (Germany and Japan)

Both of these sets are from the same shape mold. The set on the left is marked "Germany." The crude iridized floral set on *he right was made in Japan.

Canister, 2¼"	$14.00-18.00	Salt Box, 2¾"	$20.00-25.00
Canister, 3¼"	$18.00-20.00	Set, 15 Pieces	$230.00-300.00
Oil, Vinegar, 3¾"	$20.00-22.00		

Pink Floral
Dresser and Toilet Set

Chamber Pot, 2¼" $25.00-35.00
Pitcher, 5⅜"
   Bowl, 2⅛"   set $100.00-125.00
Soap Dish, 1½" x 3½" $30.00-35.00
Toothbrush
   Holder, 2" x 2½" $30.00-35.00

"Autumn"
Dresser and Toilet Set

Cold Cream Jar $35.00-45.00
Pitcher & Bowl Set $125.00-165.00
Sponge Jar $37.00-48.00
Toothbrush Holder $30.00-35.00
Waste Bowl $40.00-45.00

Wash Set
(Villeroy and Boch,
Wallerfanden)

Chamber Pot, 4¼" $75.00-90.00
Slop Jar, 7⅜" $95.00-110.00
Water Pitcher, 7¾" $95.00-110.00

Japanese and Occupied Japan Sets

Imports of Japanese children's dishes flourished between World War I and World War II. During World War II this supply was interrupted. After the war, the flood of cheap imports resumed and American-made and European products suffered severely. Between the end of World War II and April 28, 1952, the period of the American occupation, many sets were marked, "Occupied Japan." Although most of these sets lack the quality of European sets, they are highly collectible by those interested in "Occupied Japan" items.

Japanese sets may be found boxed in numerous combinations. Two-, three-, and four-place tea sets are most common. Matching dinner sets may be found in many patterns.

Otter Cocoa Set (Noritake)

Cocoa Pot and Lid	$125.00-150.00
Creamer, 2"	$45.00-50.00
Cup, 1⅝"	$27.00-32.00
Plate, 4¼"	$15.00-18.00
Saucer, 3¾"	$5.00-8.00
Sugar and Lid	$50.00-55.00
Set, 4 Places	$400.00-490.00

Noritake Tea Set

Creamer, 2½"	$15.00-18.00	Sugar and Lid, 3⅛"	$25.00-28.00
Cup, 1½"	$12.00-14.00	Teapot and Lid, 4"	$70.00-75.00
Plate, 4¾"	$6.00-8.00	Set, 6 Places	$245.00-285.00
Saucer, 4"	$4.00-5.00		

Silhouette Tea Set (Noritake)

Creamer	$15.00-18.00	Saucer, 3¾"	$4.00-5.00
Cup, 1¼"	$12.00-14.00	Teapot and Lid, 3½"	$60.00-65.00
Plate, 4¼"	$6.00-8.00	Set, 4 Places	$190.00-220.00

Bluebird Dinner Set (Noritake)

Casserole, covered, 6"	$35.00-45.00	Saucer, 3¾"	$2.00-3.00
Creamer, 1⅞"	$15.00-18.00	Sugar and Lid, 2¾"	$18.00-20.00
Cup, 1¼"	$6.00-8.00	Teapot and Lid, 3½"	$60.00-65.00
Plate, 4¼"	$5.00-8.00	Set, 4 Places	$200.00-250.00
Platter, 7⅛"	$20.00-25.00		

Floral Dinner Set
(Noritake – Made in Japan)

Casserole, covered, 6"	$25.00-30.00
Creamer, 1⅞"	$10.00-12.00
Cup, 1⅜"	$5.00-8.00
Plate, 4¼"	$4.00-5.00
Platter, 7⅛"	$12.00-14.00
Saucer, 3¾"	$3.00-4.00
Sugar and Lid, 2⅞"	$14.00-16.00
Teapot and Lid	$50.00-55.00
Set, 4 Places	$160.00-200.00

Floral Dinner Set
(Made in Japan)

Casserole, covered, 6⅝"	$12.00-14.00
Creamer, 2⅛"	$8.00-10.00
Cup, 1⅝"	$4.00-5.00
Gravy Boat, 5½"	$10.00-12.00
Plate, 5"	$3.00-4.00
Saucer, 4⅜"	$1.00-2.00
Sugar and Lid, 3⅝"	$10.00-12.00
Teapot and Lid, 3½"	$20.00-25.00
Set, 4 Places	$90.00-120.00

Chinaman Set (Japan)

Creamer, 2³⁄₁₆"	$30.00-35.00	Sugar and Lid, 2⅞"	$40.00-45.00
Cup, 1⅛"	$15.00-18.00	Teapot and Lid, 3⅝"	$65.00-75.00
Saucer, 2⅞"	$4.00-5.00	Set, 4 Places	$210.00-245.00

Floral Set (Nippon)

Creamer, 2¼"	$8.00-10.00	Sugar and Lid, 3"	$10.00-12.00
Cup, 1½"	$5.00-6.00	Teapot and Lid, 3¼"	$22.00-27.00
Plate, 5"	$4.00-5.00	Set, 4 Places	$85.00-95.00
Saucer, 4¼"	$2.00-3.00		

Blue Willow and Red Willow (Made in Japan)

Blue Willow children's dishes may be found in a variety of sizes. The photograph below shows a large-size Blue Willow dinner set. Included are the hard-to-find napkins, grill plates, 5" dinner plates, soup bowls, and an oval vegetable bowl.

The following photo includes pieces from a small-size Blue Willow dinner set and a small-size Red Willow tea set. Red Willow children's pieces are uncommon. An example of miniature Blue Willow may be seen on page 199. Sets of children's Blue Willow are commonly found in their original box. Add $20.00 to $25.00 for boxed sets.

Large Blue Willow Dinner Set

Bowl, 3½"	$35.00-40.00
Bowl, oval, 5⅜"	$35.00-40.00
Cakeplate, 5¼"	$40.00-45.00
Casserole, 4"	$40.00-45.00
Casserole 4½"	$45.00-50.00
Casserole, 5"	$45.00-50.00
Creamer, 2"	$12.00-14.00
Cup, 1½"	$8.00-10.00
Gravy Boat	$25.00-32.00
Grill Plate, 5"	$35.00-45.00
Grill Plate, 4¼"	$35.00-40.00
Knife, 4½"	$40.00-50.00
Napkins	$12.00-14.00
Plate, 5"	$14.00-16.00
Plate, 4⅜"	$5.00-8.00
Platter, 6"	$45.00-50.00
Saucer, 3¾"	$2.00-3.00
Sugar and Lid, 2¾"	$14.00-16.00
Teapot and Lid, 3¾"	$45.00-65.00

Small-size Blue Willow Dinner Set and Red Willow Tea Set

	Blue Willow	Red Willow
Casserole, 4¾"	$40.00-48.00	
Creamer, 1½"	$10.00-12.00	$25.00-30.00
Cup, 1⅛"	$8.00-9.00	$15.00-20.00
Gravy Boat	$20.00-25.00	
Plate, 3¾"	$5.00-6.00	$8.00-10.00
Platter, 4⅝"	$25.00-35.00	
Saucer, 3⅜"	$2.00-3.00	$3.00-4.00
Sugar and Lid, 2"	$16.00-18.00	$30.00-35.00
Teapot and Lid, 2⅝"	$35.00-45.00	$80.00-85.00

Real China TEA SETS
WITH FIRED·IN DECORATION

Each Toy China Tea Set is neatly packed, just as are the large sets you see in the stores, in a large beautifully designed gift box with slots to hold each piece. When not in use, the pieces can be neatly packed away.

26 Pc. Set $1.00

**Blue Willow Dinner Set
from 1930's ad.**

Phoenix Bird Tea Set (Made in Japan)

Casserole, 5¼"	$30.00-39.00
Creamer, 2⅜"	$18.00-22.00
Cup, 1⅝"	$10.00-12.00
Saucer, 4⅜"	$4.00-5.00
Sugar and Lid, 2⅞"	$28.00-32.00
Teapot and Lid, 3⅜"	$70.00-80.00
Tray, 2-H, 6¼"	$35.00-40.00
Set, 4 Places	$230.00-270.00

Snow White (c. 1937, W.D. Ent. Made in Japan)

Creamer, 2"	$25.00-28.00
Cup, 1½"	$12.00-14.00
Plate, 4⅜"	$8.00-10.00
Saucer, 2¾"	$2.00-3.00
Sugar and Lid, 2⅜"	$28.00-30.00
Teapot and Lid, 3¼"	$60.00-70.00
Set, 4 Places	$200.00-230.00

Mickey Mouse Spice Set

Canister, 1½"	$40.00-50.00
Canister, 4¼"	$100.00-125.00
Salt Box, 2¾"	$60.00-80.00
Set, 7 Pieces	$420.00-530.00

Mickey Mouse Tea Set (Copyright Walt Disney – Made in Japan)

Creamer, 2"	$20.00-22.00	Sugar and Lid, 2⅝"	$25.00-30.00
Cup, 1⅜"	$18.00-20.00	Teapot and Lid, 3½"	$80.00-90.00
Plate, 4¼"	$10.00-14.00	Tray, 6"	$25.00-30.00
Saucer, 3¾"	$3.00-4.00	Set, 4 Places	$275.00-320.00

Mickey Mouse and Little Orphan Annie (Made in Japan)

Mickey Mouse		**Little Orphan Annie**	
Creamer, 2"	$15.00-20.00	Casserole	$30.00-40.00
Cup, 1³⁄₁₆"	$15.00-18.00	Cup	$12.00-15.00
Plate, 3¼"	$8.00-10.00	Creamer	$18.00-20.00
Saucer, 3¼"	$2.00-3.00	Gravy Boat, 4½"	$25.00-30.00
Sugar and Lid, 2¾"	$20.00-25.00	Plate, 4¼"	$8.00-10.00
Teapot and Lid, 3¾"	$65.00-75.00	Platter, 5"	$14.00-16.00
Set, 4 Places	$205.00-245.00	Saucer, 3¾"	$2.00-3.00
		Sugar and Lid	$18.00-22.00
		Teapot and Lid	$45.00-55.00
		Set, 4 Places	$275.00-325.00

Mickey Mouse and Peter Pan

This Mickey Mouse set, which differs slightly from the one in the previous photo, is marked "Occupied Japan."

Mickey Mouse

Creamer	$18.00-20.00
Cup, 1³/₁₆"	$18.00-20.00
Plate, 4¾"	$8.00-10.00
Saucer, 3⅜"	$2.00-3.00
Sugar and Lid, 2¼"	$20.00-25.00
Teapot and Lid, 3¼"	$65.00-75.00
Set, 4 Places	$230.00-265.00

Peter Pan

Cup, 1³/₁₆"	$8.00-10.00
Plate, 3⅞"	$4.00-5.00
Saucer, 3½"	$1.50-2.00

Bears (Made in Japan)

The cup and saucer on the right was made in England. The cup and saucer in the foreground has "JOSEPH HORNE CO. TOY STORE" on the back of the cup.

Casserole, covered, 2¼"	$18.00-22.00	Saucer, 4¼"	$3.00-4.00
Creamer, 2½"	$14.00-16.00	Saucer, 3⅝"	$3.00-4.00
Cup, 2³/₁₆"	$12.00-15.00	Sugar and Lid	$16.00-20.00
Cup, 1⁹/₁₆"	$12.00-15.00	Cup (England), 1¾"	$15.00-16.00
Plate, 5"	$6.00-7.00	Saucer, (England), 4"	$4.00-5.00
Platter, 6¼"	$10.00-12.00		

Clown With Duck and Dog on Ball (Made in Japan)

Creamer, 1¾"	$8.00-9.00	Sugar and Lid, 2⅝"	$12.00-14.00
Cup, 1⅛"	$5.00-6.00	Teapot and Lid, 3¾"	$25.00-30.00
Plate, 3¾"	$4.00-5.00	Tray, 4¼"	$12.00-14.00
Saucer, 3⅜"	$1.50-2.00	Set, 4 Places	$100.00-115.00

"Dutch Children" (Made in Japan)

Creamer	$7.00-9.00	Sugar and Lid	$10.00-12.00
Cup	$4.00-6.00	Teapot and Lid	$22.00-27.00
Plate	$3.00-3.50	Set, 4 Places	$75.00-90.00
Saucer	$1.50-2.00		

Tan and Grey Luster Set (Phoenix China, Made in Japan)

Creamer, 2¼"	$8.00-9.00	Sugar and Lid, 2⅝"	$9.00-11.00
Cup, 1½"	$5.00-5.50	Teapot and Lid, 4"	$25.00-30.00
Plate, 3"	$4.00-4.50	Set, 4 Places	$80.00-97.00
Saucer, 2¾"	$1.00-2.00		

Tan Luster Floral Utility Set (Made in Japan)

Bowl, covered, 1⅝"	$18.00-20.00	Reamer, 2⅝"	$100.00-125.00
Casserole, oval, 1⅝"	$18.00-20.00	Shaker, pr., 1¼"	$18.00-20.00
Casserole, round, 1½"	$18.00-20.00	Salt Box, 2⅛"	$20.00-22.00
Cakeplate, 3¾"	$12.00-15.00	Spatula	$10.00-12.00
Creamer, 1½"	$8.00-10.00	Teapot and Lid, 3"	$20.00-25.00
Ice Bucket, 2⅛"	$20.00-25.00	Teapot and Lid, 2"	$18.00-22.00
Platter, 3⅞"	$10.00-12.00	Waffle Dish, 1½"	$20.00-22.00
Platter, 3⅜"	$10.00-12.00		

Octagonal-Shaped Tan Luster Utility Set (Made in Japan)

Casserole, 1¾"	$18.00-20.00	Salt Box, 2⅛"	$20.00-22.00
Ice Bucket, 2¼"	$22.00-25.00	Shaker, pr., 1½"	$18.00-20.00
Pitcher, 2¼"	$12.00-14.00	Teapot, 2¼"	$20.00-25.00
Reamer, 3¹/₁₆"	$100.00-125.00	Tray, 3"	$8.00-10.00

Elephant Luster Set (Made in Japan)

Creamer, 2"	$14.00-16.00	Sugar and Lid, 2⅜"	$20.00-25.00
Cup, ⅞"	$5.00-6.00	Teapot and Lid, 3¼"	$50.00-60.00
Saucer, 2¾"	$1.00-2.00	Set, 4 Places	$105.00-130.00

Without Luster, 50% less

Floral Boxed Tea Set

Creamer	$4.00-6.00	Sugar and Lid, 2⅛"	$5.00-8.00
Cup, ⅞"	$3.00-4.00	Teapot and Lid, 2⅝"	$14.00-16.00
Saucer, 3¼"	$1.00-1.50	Set, 2 Places	$30.00-40.00

Little Hostess Tea Set (Made in Japan)

The box is marked "Nagoya Toy Tea Set, No. 600/947, made in Japan."

Creamer, 2¼"	$8.00-9.00	Sugar and Lid, 3¼"	$12.00-14.00
Cup, 1½"	$5.00-6.00	Teapot and Lid, 3¾"	$30.00-35.00
Plate, 5"	$4.00-5.00	Set, 6 Places	$110.00-145.00
Saucer, 4¼"	$2.00-3.00		

Floral Decorated Tea Sets (Made in Japan)

Cakeplate, 4⅜"	$6.00-8.00	Saucer, 3¼"	$1.00-1.50
Creamer, 2¼"	$4.00-5.00	Sugar and Lid, 2⅝"	$6.00-8.00
Cup, 1⅛"	$2.00-3.00	Teapot and Lid, 3⅝"	$18.00-20.00
Plate, 3¾"	$2.00-2.50	Set, 4 Places	$55.00-70.00

Floral Boxed Cake Set (Japan)

Cakeplate, 4⅜"	$6.00-8.00	Saucer, 3¼"	$1.00-1.25
Creamer, 2¼"	$3.50-4.00	Sugar and Lid, 2⅝"	$4.00-6.00
Cup, 1⅛"	$2.00-2.50	Teapot and Lid, 3⅝"	$16.00-18.00
Plate, 3¾"	$2.00-2.50	Set, 4 Places	$45.00-60.00

Tan Luster Tea Sets (Made in Japan)

	Red/Blue Yellow Dots	Three Little Pigs
Creamer	$2.50-3.00	$12.00-15.00
Cup	$1.50-2.00	$6.00-8.00
Plate	$1.50-2.00	
Saucer	$1.00-1.50	$4.00-5.00
Sugar and Lid	$4.00-5.00	$15.00-18.00
Teapot and Lid	$10.00-12.00	$30.00-35.00
Set, 4 Places	$30.00-45.00	$95.00-120.00

Pagoda on White Tea Set (Made in Japan)

Creamer	$2.00-3.00	Sugar and Lid	$5.00-6.00
Cup	$1.50-2.00	Teapot and Lid	$6.00-8.00
Plate	$1.00-1.50	Set, 3 Places	$22.50-30.00
Saucer	$.75-1.00		

Bluebirds, Geisha, and Dutch Children Tea Sets (Japan)

	Bluebirds	**Geisha**	**Dutch Children**
Creamer	$8.00-9.00	$10.00-12.00	$9.00-11.00
Cup	$5.00-6.00	$6.00-8.00	$5.00-7.00
Plate	$4.00-5.00	$5.00-8.00	$5.00-6.00
Saucer	$1.00-2.00	$2.00-3.00	$1.00-2.00
Sugar and Lid	$14.00-16.00	$12.00-15.00	$12.00-14.00
Teapot and Lid	$22.00-27.00	$40.00-45.00	$30.00-35.00
Set, 4 Places	$85.00-103.00	$115.00-145.00	$95.00-120.00

Dutch Figures and Floral Tea Sets (Japan)

	Dutch Figures	**Floral**
Creamer	$8.00-10.00	$5.00-6.00
Cup	$5.00-6.00	$3.00-4.00
Plate	$4.00-5.00	$3.00-4.00
Saucer	$1.00-2.00	$1.00-2.00
Sugar and Lid	$14.00-16.00	$6.00-8.00
Teapot and Lid	$25.00-30.00	$20.00-22.00
Set, 4 Places	$90.00-110.00	$60.00-85.00

"Floral Medallion" Tea Set
(Made in Japan)

Creamer, 2¾"	$8.00-9.00
Cup, 1¾"	$3.00-4.00
Plate, 4¼"	$2.00-3.00
Saucer, 3⅛"	$1.00-2.00
Sugar and Lid, 2½"	$9.00-12.00
Teapot and Lid, 3¾"	$18.00-22.00
Set, 4 Places	$70.00-80.00

Floral Dinner Set
(Made in Japan)

Casserole	$6.00-8.00
Creamer	$4.00-5.00
Cup	$2.00-3.00
Gravy Boat	$5.00-7.00
Plate	$2.00-2.50
Platter	$3.00-4.50
Saucer	$1.00-1.25
Shaker, pr.	$5.00-8.00
Sugar and Lid	$5.00-6.00
Teapot and Lid	$8.00-10.00
Set, 4 Places	$55.00-75.00

Mieto Tea Set
(Hand painted, Made in Japan)

Creamer, 1⅞"	$4.00-5.00
Cup, 1¹⁵⁄₁₆"	$3.00-4.00
Plate, 4¾"	$2.00-3.00
Saucer, 3⅞"	$.75-1.00
Sugar and Lid, 2½"	$6.00-8.00
Teapot and Lid, 3"	$18.00-20.00
Set, 4 Places	$55.00-65.00

Ballarina (c General Ind. NY Japan)

Creamer, 2⅝"	$8.00-10.00
Cup, 1½"	$5.00-6.00
Plate, 4½"	$3.00-4.00
Saucer, 3⅛"	$1.00-1.25
Sugar and Lid, 3⅜"	$9.00-12.00
Teapot and Lid	$20.00-25.00
Set, 4 Place	$75.00-95.00

Butterfly Tea Set (Made in Japan)

Creamer, 2¼"	$8.00-9.00
Cup, 1½"	$5.00-6.00
Plate, 4⅞"	$3.00-3.50
Saucer, 4⅛"	$1.00-2.00
Sugar and Lid, 3⅛"	$10.00-12.00
Teapot and Lid, 3⅜"	$25.00-30.00
Set, 4 Places	$75.00-95.00

Mary Had A Little Lamb Teapot

This AD teapot was used by Canonsburg to produce a child's set. For shapes of the other pieces in the set see the photo of the "Hunter with the Dog."

Teapot and Lid, 6¼" $55.00-65.00

"Hunter with Dog" (Canonsburg Pottery Co.)

	Hunter with Dog	Mary Had A Little Lamb
Creamer	$10.00-12.00	$12.00-15.00
Cup	$7.00-8.00	$7.00-9.00
Plate	$4.00-5.00	$5.00-8.00
Saucer	$2.00-3.00	$2.00-3.00
Sugar	$10.00-12.00	$12.00-15.00
Teapot and Lid, 6¼"	$45.00-55.00	$55.00-65.00
Set, 4 Places	$115.00-140.00	$135.00-170.00

"Circus" Tea Set (Edwin M. Knowles China Company)

Creamer, 2⅛"	$8.00-10.00	Sugar, 2⅛"	$8.00-10.00
Cup, 2⅛"	$6.00-7.00	Teapot and Lid, 4½"	$30.00-35.00
Plate, 6½"	$4.00-5.00	Set, 4 Places	$90.00-110.00
Saucer, 4¾"	$2.00-2.50		

Tea Sets by Edwin M. Knowles China Co.

	Dutch Figures	Floral
Creamer, 2⅛"	$10.00-12.00	$6.00-8.00
Cup, 2⅛"	$6.00-7.00	$4.00-5.00
Plate, 5¼"	$4.00-6.00	$2.00-3.00
Saucer, 4¾"	$2.00-3.00	$1.00-1.50
Sugar, 2⅛"	$10.00-12.00	$6.00-8.00
Teapot and Lid, 4⅝"	$40.00-50.00	$30.00-35.00
Set, 4 Places	$90.00-120.00	$70.00-90.00

"Playful Zoo Animals" (Edwin M. Knowles China Co.)

Creamer, 2¾"	$8.00-10.00	Sugar and Lid, 2¾"	$12.00-16.00
Cup, 2¼"	$6.00-7.00	Teapot and Lid, 3½"	$40.00-50.00
Plate, 6½"	$4.00-6.00	Set, 4 Places	$105.00-130.00
Saucer, 5¼"	$2.00-3.00		

Pastel Blue Rib and Floral Set (K.T.&K.)

Bowl, berry	$5.00-6.00	Platter, 7¾"	$14.00-16.00
Bowl, oval, 5⅝"	$17.00-19.00	Saucer, 5⅛"	$2.00-3.00
Casserole, 5½"	$27.50-30.00	Sugar and Lid, 3"	$14.00-16.00
Creamer, 2¼"	$10.00-12.00	Teapot and Lid, 3¼"	$35.00-45.00
Cup, 2⅛"	$6.00-7.00	Set, 4 Places	$175.00-210.00
Plate, 6"	$5.00-6.00		

Bluebird Child's Set (K.T.&K. China)

This set which includes dinnerware pieces was produced by Knowles, Taylor and Knowles of East Liverpool, Ohio. Notice the dinner plates and saucers are 12-sided.

Bowl, oval, 5⅝"	$22.00-25.00	Platter, 7¾"	$18.00-20.00
Casserole, 5½"	$40.00-45.00	Saucer, 5⅛"	$4.00-5.00
Creamer, 2¼"	$10.00-12.00	Sugar and Lid, 3"	$16.00-20.00
Cup, 2⅛"	$7.00-9.00	Teapot and Lid, 3¼"	$45.00-55.00
Plate, 6"	$6.00-8.00	Set, 4 Places	$220.00-265.00

Old Moss Rose

Creamer	$15.00-18.00	Sugar and Lid	$20.00-25.00
Cup	$6.00-8.00	Teapot and Lid	$45.00-55.00
Plate	$5.00-7.00	Set, 4 Places	$135.00-170.00
Saucer	$2.00-3.00		

Morning Glory

Creamer	$15.00-17.00	Sugar and Lid	$20.00-25.00
Cup	$7.00-9.00	Teapot and Lid	$45.00-55.00
Plate	$5.00-7.00	Set, 4 Places	$150.00-175.00
Saucer	$3.00-3.50		

Basket (Basket P. P. Salem China Co.)

Creamer, 2¼"	$6.00-7.00	Saucer, 4⅝"	$1.00-2.00
Cup, 2"	$6.00-7.00	Sugar, 2¼"	$6.00-7.00
Plate, 6¼"	$4.00-5.00	Teapot and Lid	$40.00-50.00
Plate, 2-H, 8"	$10.00-12.00	Set, 4 Places	$110.00-130.00

Salem China Co. Child's Set

Creamer, 2¼"	$6.00-7.00	Saucer, 4⅝"	$1.00-2.00
Cup, 2"	$6.00-7.00	Sugar, 2¼"	$6.00-7.00
Plate, 6¼"	$4.00-5.00	Teapot and Lid	$45.00-55.00
Plate, 2-H, 8"	$12.00-15.00	Set, 4 Places	$110.00-140.00

Salem China Co. Child's Sets

The Little Bo Peep set on the right was called "Victory." The set on the left is marked "Godey Prints."

	Godey Prints	Victory
Creamer, 2¼"	$6.00-7.00	$6.00-8.00
Cup, 2"	$6.00-7.00	$7.00-9.00
Plate, 6¼"	$4.00-5.00	$5.00-6.00
Plate, 2-H, 8"	$10.00-12.00	$15.00-17.00
Saucer, 4⅝"	$1.00-2.00	$2.00-3.00
Sugar, 2¼"	$6.00-7.00	$6.00-8.00
Teapot and Lid	$40.00-45.00	$50.00-55.00
Set, 4 Places	$105.00-125.00	$135.00-160.00

Minuet (Salem China Co.)

This set depicts a man and woman in Colonial dress with the man bowing to the woman.

Creamer, 2¼"	$6.00-7.00	Saucer, 4⅝"	$1.00-2.00
Cup, 2"	$6.00-7.00	Sugar, 2¼"	$6.00-7.00
Plate, 6¼"	$4.00-5.00	Teapot and Lid	$40.00-50.00
Plate, 2-H, 8"	$12.00-14.00	Set, 4 Places	$110.00-135.00

CHILD'S FINE AMERICAN SEVENTEEN-PIECE TEA SET

She'll be a proud hostess when she serves with this beautifully shaped tea set . . . that looks just like mother's! Smooth, non-cracking glaze protects a colonial lady and gentleman in pastel Pink and Blue costumes, encircled by a garland of Pink roses. Rich, Ivory-toned background; 23-Karat Gold border design. Set contains: 4 cups, 4 saucers, 4 six-inch plates, 1 seven-inch cake plate, covered teapot, sugar bowl and creamer.

81221 B475 Child's 17-Piece Tea Set—Service for Four . . $6.75

Minuet scene on another china blank from the John Plain Book, 1949.

"Gumdrop Tree" (Southern Potteries, Erwin, TN)

Creamer, 3"	$20.00-27.00	Sugar, 2"	$20.00-27.00
Cup, 2¼"	$20.00-27.00	Teapot and Lid, 6½"	$75.00-90.00
Plate, 6"	$10.00-14.00	Set, 4 Places	$250.00-325.00
Saucer, 4½"	$4.00-5.00		

"Whirligig" (Southern Potteries, Erwin, TN)

Creamer, 3"	$22.00-28.00	Sugar, 2"	$18.00-20.00
Cup, 2¼"	$20.00-27.00	Teapot and Lid, 6½"	$75.00-85.00
Plate, 6"	$8.00-10.00	Set, 4 Places	$245.00-300.00
Saucer, 4½"	$4.00-5.00		

"Daffodil" (Southern Potteries, Erwin, TN)

Creamer, 3"	$18.00-20.00	Sugar, 2"	$18.00-20.00
Cup, 2¼"	$20.00-25.00	Teapot and Lid, 6½"	$70.00-80.00
Plate, 6"	$8.00-10.00	Set, 4 Places	$230.00-275.00
Saucer, 4½"	$3.00-4.00		

Warwick Floral (Warwick, Made in U.S.A.)

This set was made in the mid-1940's by the
Warwick China Company of Wheeling, West Virginia.

Creamer, 2¾"	$5.00-9.00	Sugar and Lid, 3½"	$5.00-8.00
Cup, 1¾"	$6.00-7.00	Teapot and Lid, 5"	$40.00-45.00
Plate, 6¼"	$4.00-5.00	Set, 4 Places	$100.00-125.00
Saucer, 4⅞"	$2.00-3.00		

Warwick China Child's Tea Set

This set appears to have a combination of decals. "Mary Had A Little Lamb" and "Hunter with a Dog" are the two dominant themes. Both of these decals were also used on children's dishes produced by other companies.

Creamer, 2¾"	$8.00-10.00
Cup, 1¾"	$7.00-8.00
Plate, 6¼"	$5.00-6.00
Saucer, 4⅞"	$2.00-3.00
Sugar and Lid, 3½"	$10.00-15.00
Teapot and Lid, 5"	$55.00-65.00
Set, 4 Places	$130.00-160.00

Miscellaneous China

"Waterfront Scenes"

This set is unmarked. The shape is similar to both American and English sets.

Creamer, 3⅝"	$6.00-8.00	Sugar and Lid, 4⅛"	$8.00-10.00
Cup, 2¼"	$5.00-6.00	Teapot and Lid, 4¼"	$20.00-25.00
Plate, 5¼"	$4.00-4.50	Waste Bowl	$12.00-15.00
Saucer, 4¾"	$1.00-1.50	Set, 4 Places	$85.00-105.00

"Orange Twin Flower" (Unmarked)

Creamer, 3⅝"	$5.00-6.00	Sugar and Lid, 3½"	$6.00-10.00
Cup, 2¼"	$4.00-5.00	Teapot and Lid, 6¼"	$22.00-27.00
Plate, 4⅞"	$4.00-5.00	Set, 4 Places	$70.00-90.00
Saucer, 4⅞"	$1.00-2.00		

Polka Dot Tea Set

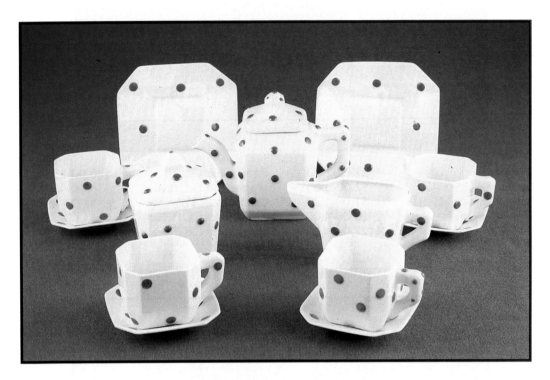

Creamer, 2½"	$6.00-9.00	Sugar and Lid, 3¾"	$10.00-12.50
Cup, 2"	$4.00-6.00	Teapot and Lid, 4¼"	$22.00-27.00
Plate, 4½"	$4.00-5.00	Set, 4 Places	$75.00-100.00
Saucer, 3⅛"	$1.50-2.00		

Rose Border Dinner Set

This dinner set is of European manufacture, but the set is unmarked and its country of origin is uncertain.

Casserole, 5"	$25.00-30.00	Plate, 4½"	$5.00-6.00
Gravy Boat/Underplate	$25.00-30.00	Platter, 4½"	$15.00-18.00
Plate, 4"	$5.00-6.00	Platter, 5"	$15.00-18.00

**Scottie Dog Feeding Dish
(Harker Pottery)**

Bowl, 7" $35.00-45.00

Harker Pottery Company Children's Dishes

Mug, 3" $18.00-20.00   Plate, 7¾" $18.00-20.00   Warmer Bowl, 9" $25.00-32.00

Plate, divided, 9":
  Halloween – $35.00-45.00
  Circus Animals – $25.00-28.00

Miniature Ironstone

Creamer	$2.00-2.50	Plate, (Blue Onion)	$20.00-25.00
Cup	$2.00-3.00	Teapot and Lid, (Swan)	$30.00-40.00
Plate	$1.00-1.25	Cup (Floral), 3¾"	$2.00-4.00
Sugar and Lid	$3.00-4.00	Saucer (Floral), 1½"	$1.00-1.50
Teapot and Lid	$12.00-14.00	Teapot and Lid (Floral), 3⅛"	$14.00-16.00

China Miniatures

Candelabrum, 3-branch, 2½"	$30.00-35.00
Chamberstick, German, front left	$25.00-30.00
Chamberstick, Dresden, rear left	$60.00-75.00
Cheese Dish, 2½"	$75.00-85.00
Chocolate Pot, German, 5"	$85.00-95.00
Chocolate Pot, enameled, 3"	$57.00-65.00
Creamer, Shelley	$40.00-50.00
Cup and saucer, Shelley	$60.00-75.00

Dresser Set

Hair Receiver, 1¾"	$27.00-30.00
Pin Tray	$17.00-19.00
Hat Pin Holder, 2¾"	$27.00-30.00
Powder Box, 1¾"	$27.00-30.00
Set, 4 Pieces	$100.00-110.00
Pitcher & Bowl, Gaudy Welsh-type	$145.00-175.00

Food

The china food above is shown served on ironstone, glass, metal, and paper dishes. The pieces range in price from $20.00 to about $60.00. Fancy ironstone pieces are the most expensive and paper serving pieces are the least valuable.

Full-Size Children's Dishes

Davy Crockett

Front Row:
1. Bowl, "Davy Crockett Frontiersman," 6" $25.00-28.00;
2. Plate, "Davy Crockett," 7¼" $18.00-20.00;
3. Bowl, "Davy Crockett," 6¼" $22.00-25.00;

Center Row:
1. Plate, "Davy Crockett Frontiersman," 9¼" $22.00-25.00;
2. Mug, "The Big Bear Hunter," 3⅛" $20.00-22.00;
3. Plate, Davy Crockett with a Bear (W.S. George), 9¼" $20.00-25.00;

Back Row:
1. Plate, "Davy Crockett" (Royal China), 9½" $25.00-30.00;
2. Plate, "Davy Crockett" (The Oxford China Co.), 9½" $25.00-30.00

Miscellaneous Baby Dishes

Front Row:
1. Mug, "Cowboy Dog," (Knowles China Co.), 2⅞" $14.00-16.00;
2. Mug, "Peter Cottontail" (Homer Laughlin Co.), 3" $30.00-35.00;
3. Hopalong Cassidy Utensils, boxed set $35.00-45.00;
4. Hopalong Cassidy Bowl, 5⅜" $30.00-35.00;

Back Row:
1. Plate, "Children at Play" (Knowles China Co.), 6⅞" $16.00-18.00;
2. Baby Dish, "Jack and Jill" $15.00-18.00;
3. "Sunbonnet Babies" ABC Plate, 6¼" $30.00-40.00

Miscellaneous Baby Dishes

Front Row:
1. Bowl, "Tom Tom the Piper's Son," 5⅜" $14.00-16.00;
2. Mug, "Hickory, Dickory, Dock," 2⅝" $12.00-15.00;
3. Mug, "Little Boy Blue," 3" $14.00-18.00;

Center Row:
1. Mug, "Tom Tom the Piper's Son," 2⅝" $12.00-14.00;
2. Plate, "Betsy McCall's Friends," $40.00-50.00;

Back Row:
1. Plate, "Little Jack Horner," 7¼" $12.00-14.00;
2. Mug, "Betsy McCall's Friends," $12.00-14.00

Nursery Rhyme Scenes

Front Row:
1. Mug, "Mary Had A Little Lamb," 2⅝" $12.00-14.00;
2. Bowl, "Little Bo Peep," 5¼" $12.00-14.00;

Back Row:
1. Plate, divided "Animals" $14.00-16.00;
2. Bowl, "Elsie," 9⅛" $25.00-35.00;
3. Plate, "Mary Had A Little Lamb," 7¼" $10.00-12.00

Hot Plate and Cover (Majestic Products)

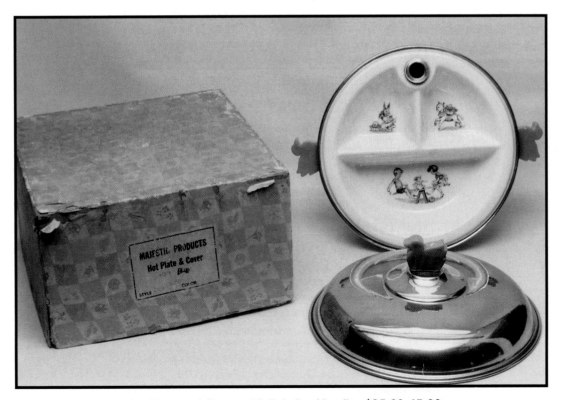

Hot Plate and Cover with Bakelite Handles $35.00-45.00

Plates, Mugs, and Bowls

Front Row:
1. Mug, "Playful Dog" (Warwick China), 2⅞" $15.00-18.00;
2. Mug, "Little Boy Blue," 2⅝" $12.00-18.00;
3. Plate, "Peter Pumpkin Eater," 7¼" $10.00-12.00;

Center Row:
1. Bowl, "Little Miss Muffet," 5¾" $10.00-12.00;
2. Mug, "Raggedy Ann," 2⅝" $14.00-16.00;

Back Row:
1. Plate, "Jack Be Nimble," 7¼" $8.00-10.00;
2. Plate, "See-Saw Margery Daw," $10.00-12.00;
3. Mug, "Ride a Cock Horse," $10.00-12.00

Shenango China

Front Row:
1. Bowl, "Little Tommy Tucker," 5¾" $10.00-15.00;
2. Mug, "Little Bo Peep," 2⅞" $18.00-20.00;
3. Plate, "Little Miss Muffet," 6" $5.00-8.00;
4. Bowl, "Jack Be Quick," 5½" $8.00-10.00;

Back Row:
1. Plate, "Little Bo Peep," 9" $14.00-18.00;
2. Plate, "Mistress Mary," 7" $10.00-15.00;
3. Plate, "Jack Be Nimble," 9" $14.00-18.00

Plate and Mug Sets

"Children Fishing" (Noritake)
Bowl, 5⅞" $30.00-35.00;
Mug, 2½" $25.00-30.00;
Plate, 7¼" $18.00-22.00;
Set, 3 pieces $75.00-87.00

**"Barnyard Scenes"
(Royal Windsor, England)**
Bowl, 5⅜" $12.00-15.00;
Mug, 3¼" $18.00-20.00;
Plate, 8" $18.00-20.00;
Set, 3 pieces $48.00-55.00

"Red Riding Hood"
Mug, 3½" $18.00-20.00;
Plate, 7" $10.00-12.00;
Set, 2 pieces $28.00-32.00

Noritake Child's Set

Bowl, 5¾" $30.00-35.00
Mug, 2⅝" $25.00-30.00

Plate, 7¾" $20.00-25.00
Set, 3 pieces $75.00-90.00

China Mugs

Tom Tom	$12.00-14.00
Circus Clown	$12.00-14.00
Mary Had A Little Lamb	$15.00-18.00
Tom Tom ABC	$12.00-14.00

German Baby Dishes

Left:
   "North Pole Discovered by Pooh – Pooh Found It."
Backstamped – "Bavaria – Schuman – A.M. Milna –
Winnie The Pooh – Made in Germany," 8" $50.00-60.00.

Right:
   Divided bowl with three scenes – Little Molly
Flanders; The sheep's in the meadow, the cow's in the
corn; Ole King Cole, 8" $35.00-40.00.

Baby Plate, Zona Strutting Duck,
7" rolled edge $60.00-70.00
Mug, Zona Strutting Duck, 3" $50.00-60.00

Ralston Purina Bowl

Bowl, Ralston Purina, 6" $35.00-45.00

**Scottie Dog Feeding Dish
(Harker Pottery)**

Bowl, 7" $35.00-45.00

Harker Pottery Company Children's Dishes

Mug, 3" $18.00-20.00   Plate, 7¾" $18.00-20.00   Warmer Bowl, 9" $25.00-32.00

Plate, divided, 9":
Halloween – $35.00-45.00
Circus Animals – $25.00-28.00

Baby Dishes

Mug, Hankscraft, 3" $15.00-20.00
Warmer Bowl, Hankscraft, divided, 9" $25.00-30.00
Warmer Bowl, Hunt Scene, 7" $35.00-40.00

Bunnykins (Royal Doulton)

Bowl $25.00-35.00
Mug $25.00-35.00
Plate $25.00-35.00
The prices above are for older sets.
New Royal Doulton Bunnykins sets may still be purchased.

Divided Plate

Plate, divided, 7"
$25.00-30.00

Bears ABC Plate

Plate, Smith-Phillips Semi-Porcelain, 7"
$50.00-60.00

Roseville Dishes

Bowl (Rabbits)	$80.00-90.00
Creamer (Rabbit)	$90.00-110.00
Mug (Rabbit)	$80.00-90.00
Mug (Dutch Girl)	$100.00-125.00
Plate (Rabbits)	$80.00-90.00
Plate (Children)	$75.00-85.00

Creamer $65.00-85.00   Sugar and Lid $80.00-90.00   Teapot and Lid $150.00-175.00

Big Circus Breakfast Set

This set is backstamped "The California Cleminsons." Bowl, 4⅝"; Sugar, 7¾"; Waffle Dish, 8¼"
Set, 3 Pieces $30.00-40.00

Miniature Rolling Pins

Rolling Pin (Mary Had A Little Lamb), 9"	$145.00-165.00
Rolling Pins with advertising	$65.00-85.00
Rolling Pins with no decal	$18.00-22.00

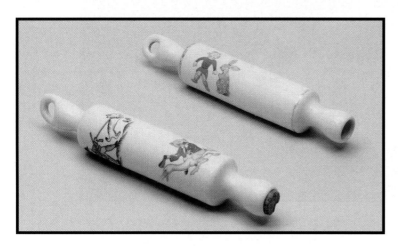

Rolling Pin
   (Boy with Pink Rabbit), 9" $125.00-150.00
Rolling Pin (Three Scenes) –
   Elephant on Roller Skates;
   Hunter with Dog;
   Pig Riding a Goose, 9" $145.00-155.00

Kitty Bank

Pig Bank

Pig Bank
(Mary Had A Little Lamb Decal)
$60.00-75.00

Kitty Bank
(Mary Had A Little Lamb Decal)
$55.00-65.00

Baby Reamers

Top Row:
    1. $65.00-85.00; 2. $75.00-90.00; 3. $50.00-65.00
Center Row:
    1. $55.00-65.00; 2. $75.00-85.00
Bottom Row:
    1. $75.00-85.00; 2. $75.00-85.00; 3. $50.00-55.00

Baby Reamers

Top Row:
    1. $70.00-90.00; 2. $60.00-75.00; 3. $40.00-45.00
Center Row:
    1. $75.00-80.00; 2. $50.00-65.00
Bottom Row:
    1. $80.00-90.00

PART 3: STONEWARE, METAL AND PLASTIC

Miniature Steins and Jugs

The brown earthenware steins are marked "Germany" around the top rim. The blue and white pitcher on the top row is marked "Wedgewood, Made in England." The mug on the top row, right side is Royal Doulton. The stein in the center row on the right is marked "Doulton, Lambeth, England."

Top Row:
    1. (3¾") $145.00-185.00   2. (3⅜") $27.00-32.00
    3. (2") $35.00-45.00   4. (2") $57.00-62.00
    5. (1⅞") 45.00-50.00   6. (2⅜") $90.00-110.00

Center Row:
    1. (2¼") $35.00-40.00   2. (1¾") $30.00-35.00
    3. (1¾") $25.00-30.00   4. (1¾") $25.00-30.00
    5. (1¼") $60.00-65.00   6. (2") $35.00-40.00
    7. (1⅞") $75.00-90.00

Bottom Row:
    1. (1⁵⁄₁₆") $45.00-50.00   2. (1⁷⁄₁₆") $45.00-50.00
    3. (1⅛") $37.00-47.00   4. (1⅜") $8.00-10.00
    5. (1⅞") $18.00-22.00   6. (1½") $18.00-22.00
    7. (1⅝") $12.00-14.00   8. (1⅝") $37.00-42.00

Miniature Stoneware Bowls and Pie Plates

Many of the pieces shown in this photo were used as salesman's samples. The measurements represent height. The diameters range from 2" to 3¼".

Top Row:
1. (1¾") $18.00-22.00
2. (1¾") $18.00-22.00
3. (1⅝") $50.00-60.00
4. (1¾") $50.00-60.00

Center Row:
1. (¾") $14.00-18.00
2. (¾") $16.00-20.00
3. (¾") $28.00-35.00
4. (1") $18.00-20.00
5. (1¼") $27.00-35.00
6. (1¼") $27.00-35.00

Bottom Row:
1. (1½") $60.00-67.00
2. (1¼") $27.00-35.00
3. (1⅛") $35.00-40.00

Miniature Stoneware

Top Row:
1. Bean Pot, (2¾") $40.00-50.00
2. Spittoon, (2½") $50.00-65.00
3. Bean Pot, (2¾") $40.00-50.00

Center Row:
1. Pitcher, (1⅝") $18.00-22.00
2. Pitcher, (1½") $18.00-22.00
3. Covered Pot, "Bohemian," (2½") $45.00-55.00
4. Flask, (1⅝") $14.00-18.00
5. Crock, "Boston Baked Beans"(1¾") $20.00-22.00
6. Jug, "Diamond Club Pure Rye Whiskey,"(1")
   With advertising $100.00-135.00
   Without advertising $18.00-22.00
7. Crock, (1⅝") $25.00-30.00

Bottom Row:
1.-4. (1⅛") $15.00-18.00
5.-7. Pitchers, (1½") $18.00-22.00

Aluminum and Tinware

*Pan, 1¼"	$10.00-12.00
*Pan, 1½"	$10.00-12.00
*Pot, 2-handle, 1½"	$12.00-14.00
*Pot, 2-handle, 2"	$12.00-14.00
*Skillet, 1⅛"	$10.00-12.00
Funnel	$8.00-10.00
Funnel, 2¼"	$8.00-9.00
Tool Set, 4 Pieces	$50.00-55.00
Cocoa Tin	$50.00-55.00

*Entire set has been reproduced.

Graniteware

"Frolicking Children" Graniteware Tea Set (Made in Germany)

Creamer, 2½"	$40.00-50.00	Sugar, 2½"	$40.00-50.00
Cup, 1⅝"	$28.00-35.00	Teapot and Lid, 3½"	$120.00-135.00
Saucer, 3½"	$5.00-6.00	Set, 6 Places	$400.00-480.00

"Her Pet" Graniteware Tea Set

Creamer	$32.00-37.00
Cup	$20.00-25.00
Saucer	$4.00-6.00
Sugar	$40.00-45.00
Teapot and Lid	$100.00-120.00
Set, 4 Places	$270.00-325.00

Blue Graniteware Tea Set

Creamer	$28.00-30.00
Cup	$18.00-20.00
Saucer	$4.00-5.00
Sugar	$28.00-30.00
Teapot and Lid	$85.00-90.00
Set, 4 Place	$230.00-250.00

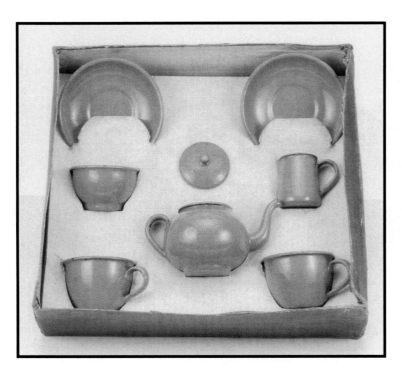

Blue Graniteware Tea Set

This 2-place graniteware tea set is still in its original box. The box is marked "Made in Germany."

Creamer, 2"	$22.00-27.00
Cup, 2"	$18.00-20.00
Saucer, 4"	$4.00-5.00
Sugar, 1¾"	$22.00-27.00
Teapot and Lid, 2¾"	$95.00-110.00
Set, 2 Places	$185.00-215.00

Blue Speckled Graniteware Tea Set

Creamer	$32.00-37.00
Cup	$25.00-30.00
Saucer	$4.00-5.00
Sugar and Lid	$40.00-45.00
Teapot and Lid	$115.00-125.00
Set, 4 Places	$300.00-350.00

Graniteware Tea Sets

	Blue	White with Blue Band
Creamer	$32.00-35.00	$28.00-32.00
Cup	$18.00-20.00	$15.00-16.00
Saucer	$4.00-5.00	$4.00-5.00
Sugar	$25.00-30.00	$22.00-28.00
Teapot and Lid	$70.00-75.00	$70.00-75.00
Set, 4 Places	$215.00-235.00	$195.00-220.00

Blue Banded Graniteware Tea Set with Gold Trim

Creamer, 2¼"	$30.00-35.00
Cup, 2¾"	$20.00-22.00
Plate, 5⅛"	$10.00-12.00
Saucer, 4¼"	$4.00-5.00
Sugar and Lid, 2½"	$37.00-42.00
Teapot and Lid, 5"	$100.00-120.00
Set, 6 Places	$375.00-430.00

Blue Granite Tea Set

Creamer	$30.00-35.00	Sugar and Lid	$37.00-42.00
Cup	$18.00-20.00	Teapot and Lid	$90.00-100.00
Saucer	$4.00-5.00	Set, 4 Places	$250.00-275.00

Blue Granite Kitchenware

Sugar (Blue & White)	$20.00-25.00
Sugar (Light Blue)	$20.00-25.00
Sugar (Dark Blue)	$25.00-30.00
Funnel	$45.00-55.00
Scoop	$60.00-65.00
Tray, 2-H	$35.00-40.00

Blue Granite Kitchenware

Ladle	$30.00-35.00	Strainer (deep)	$30.00-45.00
Pan	$35.00-40.00	Skillet	$35.00-40.00
Strainer	$30.00-40.00		

Blue Speckled Granite Kitchenware

The egg fryer pictured in the left foreground should have a handle.

Casserole, covered, 2⅞"	$100.00-125.00	Milk Pitcher, 2½"	$75.00-85.00
Egg Fryer	$80.00-90.00	Mold, ruffled, 2¾"	$65.00-85.00
Frying Pan, 4½"	$60.00-75.00	Mug, 1⅝"	$55.00-65.00
Grater, 4"	$85.00-95.00	Plate, 2⅜"	$25.00-30.00
Ladle, 4¼"	$40.00-50.00		

Light Blue Speckled Granite Kitchenware

Ladle, 4½"	$35.00-40.00
Pan, 4¼"	$42.00-47.00
Skillet, 4¼"	$37.00-40.00
Spoon, 3¼"	$30.00-35.00
Strainer, 4½"	$35.00-40.00
Tray, 2-H, 4⅝"	$45.00-50.00

Gray Speckled Granite Kitchenware

Funnel, 2¼"	$60.00-70.00	Roaster with spout, 4"	$85.00-95.00
Grater, 4½"	$85.00-90.00	Skillet, 5½"	$50.00-60.00
Ladle, 4⅜"	$40.00-50.00	Skillet, 5⅜"	$50.00-60.00
Mold, ruffled, 2¾"	$65.00-85.00	Strainer, 4⅜"	$40.00-50.00
Pan, 2-H, 2"	$85.00-100.00		

Graniteware Accessories

The bucket is a mottled blue color and the colander is gray speckled. The other two items are pale blue.

Colander, 1¼"	$85.00-90.00
Ice Bucket	$145.00-160.00
Soap Dish, 1¾" x 2¾"	$45.00-55.00
Slop Jar, 2¾"	$80.00-90.00

Pink Granite Chamber Accessories

Chamber Stick $65.00-85.00
Potty $40.00-50.00
Slop Jar $75.00-85.00

Graniteware Mickey Mouse Child's Bowl

Bowl, Mickey Mouse
with Giant Mushroom
$100.00-125.00

Miscellaneous Graniteware

The blue and white and green and white pieces at the far right are not actually graniteware, but are graniteware look-alikes. The mottled design on these pieces is painted over the metal base.

	Bowl	**Bucket**	**Plate**
Green/White	$18.00-20.00	$18.00-20.00	$8.00-10.00
Lt. Blue/White	$20.00-22.00	$20.00-22.00	$9.00-11.00
Dark Blue		$100.00-125.00	
Gray	$25.00-30.00		
Cream	$20.00-25.00		
Blue /White	$40.00-50.00		
Blue/White Inside	$40.00-45.00		

	Teapot	**Sauce Pan**
Green/White	$35.00-40.00	$18.00-20.00
Lt. Blue/White	$37.00-42.00	$18.00-20.00

	Potty	**Rectangular Baker**
Gray		$40.00-45.00
Lavender	$125.00-145.00	

Graniteware Toy Mold Set

Set, 11 Pieces $200.00-225.00

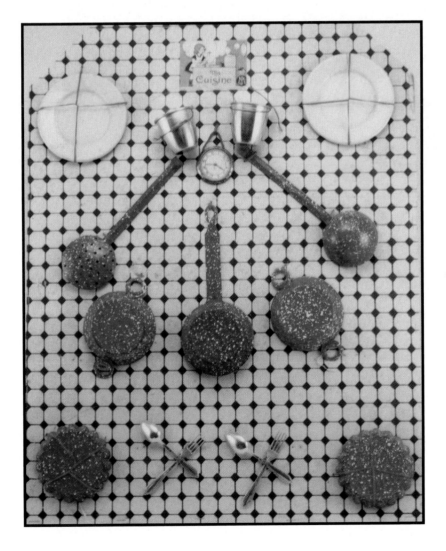

Ma Cuisine Kitchenware

This set is composed of red speckled granite look-alike pieces.

Set, $145.00-165.00

Copper and Brass

Top Row:
    1. Copper Pans, 3-piece set $75.00-90.00
    3. Coffee Grinder, 2" $45.00-65.00
Center Row:
    1. Teapot, 2¾" $75.00-85.00
    3. Teapot, (Holland), 2¼" $35.00-45.00
    5. Blue & White handled silverware ea. $18.00-20.00
Bottom Row:
    1. Strainer, 5" $22.00-25.00
    3. Scoop, 5" $20.00-22.00
    5. Rolling Pin, 4¼" $20.00-25.00

2. Mortar and Pestle, $25.00-30.00
4. "Daisy" Coffee Grinder, 3" $100.00-125.00

2. Teapot, (England), 2¼" $60.00-70.00
4. Copper Mold, 2" $30.00-35.00

2. Potato Masher, 3½" $16.00-18.00
4. Scoop, 3" $25.00-27.00

Pewter Tea Set

Creamer, 3¼"	$28.00-35.00	Spooner, 2⅝"	$35.00-40.00
Cup, 1⅜"	$20.00-22.00	Sugar and Lid, 3½"	$37.00-45.00
Saucer, 3⅝"	$4.00-6.00	Teapot and Lid, 4½"	$50.00-70.00
Spoon, 3¼"	$5.00-7.00	Set, 4 Places	$265.00-330.00

Miscellaneous Pewter

Tea Set

Creamer, 2⅜"	$20.00-22.00	Castor Set, 2½"	$90.00-110.00
Cup, 2⅞"	$15.00-18.00	Castor Set, 2"	$75.00-80.00
Saucer, 2"	$4.00-5.00	Hot Water Bottle, 2¼"	$45.00-50.00
Sugar and Lid, 2½"	$28.00-35.00	Plate, 2⅛"	$10.00-12.00
Teapot and Lid, 3½"	$37.00-45.00	Scissors, 2"	$18.00-20.00
Set, 4 Places	$160.00-195.00	Spoon, 1½"	$3.00-4.00
		Syrup, 4¾"	$85.00-125.00
		Tray, 2¼" x 3"	$18.00-20.00

Pewter Tableware

Set, 6 Places $110.00-125.00

Tinware

Box	$65.00-70.00	Plate, Bicycles	$60.00-65.00
Colander	$25.00-30.00	Plate, Horse	$115.00-120.00
Funnel	$8.00-10.00	Plate, Lion	$110.00-120.00
Grater	$22.00-25.00	Salt Box	$35.00-40.00
Muffin Pan	$15.00-18.00	Scoop	$15.00-18.00
Pail, handled	$50.00-55.00	Seive	$20.00-22.00
Pie Tin	$7.50-10.00	Sifter	$75.00-85.00

Tinware

Cookie Sheet	$25.00-28.00	Plate, enameled	$10.00-14.00
Dust Pan	$8.00-10.00	Strainer, large	$15.00-18.00
Hamburger Holder	$10.00-12.00	Strainer, small	$20.00-22.00
Nut Pan	$35.00-40.00	Teapot	$30.00-40.00
Pie Plate	$4.00-6.00	Tool Set	$45.00-47.00
Plate	$6.00-8.00		

Griswold Cookware (Griswold, Erie, PA)

Casserole, oval, 6"	$300.00-350.00
Corn Mold, 4⅛" x 8½"	$65.00-75.00
Kettle, covered, 4¾"	$85.00-90.00
Skillet, 4⅜"	$75.00-85.00

Wagner Ware

The three pieces on the left and the small skillet in the foreground are not Wagner.

Griddle, 4½"	$100.00-125.00
Corn Mold (Griswold), 4½" x 8½"	$65.00-75.00
Skillet (unmarked) 3⅝"	$18.00-22.00
Teapot (unmarked) 2⅛"	$85.00-100.00
Waffle Iron (Freidag Mfg. Co.), 4¼"	$100.00-125.00
*Kettle, covered, 3"	$80.00-100.00
*Kettle, open, 2½"	$45.00-50.00
*Skillet, 4⅜"	$45.00-50.00
*Teapot, 3¾"	$150.00-185.00
*Boxed Set, 4 Pieces	$320.00-385.00

Tootsietoy Tea Set

Tootsietoy Tea Set $65.00-85.00

Miniature Cookware

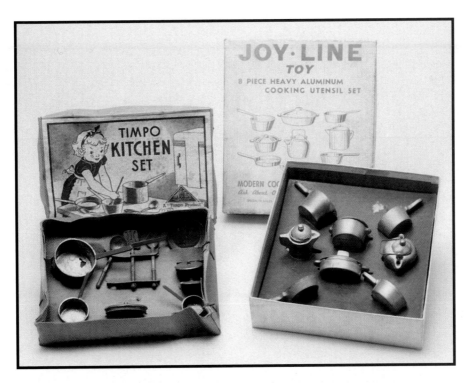

The Timpo Kitchen Set was made by Timpo Toys of England. It consists of three heavy metal covered pots, a skillet, and three serving utensils. Specialty Sales Corporation of St. Louis, Missouri, marketed The Joy Line Toys Cooking Utensil set. This is an eight-piece heavy aluminum cookware set consisting of three sizes of open pots, a covered oval casserole, a round covered casserole, a coffee pot, a skillet, and a covered tea pot.

Joy Line Toys Set	$55.00-65.00
Timpo Kitchen Set	$45.00-50.00

Metal Cookware Set

Pan, open, 6½"	$35.00-40.00
Pot, covered, 5"	$45.00-55.00
Skillet, 6½"	$45.00-55.00

Metal Tableware

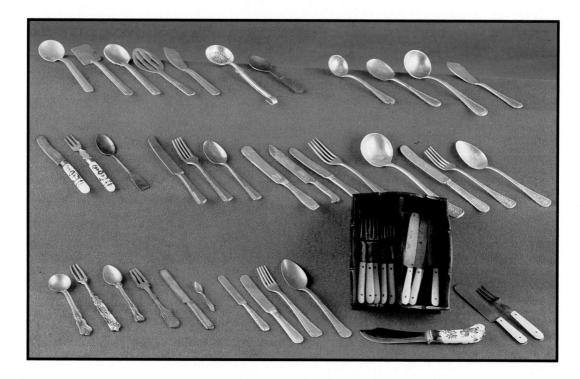

	Pewter	Bone Handle	Blue Handle	Austria/ Germany	U.S.A. Unmarked
Silverware	$2.00-2.50	$10.00-12.00	$10.00-12.00	$2.00-2.50	$1.00-1.50

Serving pieces, add 50%

Wear-Ever Cookware Set No. 251

Wear-Ever "Hallite Junior" Cookware Set

This set was marketed by the Wolverine Aluminum Ware Company of Pittsburgh, Pennsylvania. "Hallite" is a trademark of the Aluminum Cooking Utensil Company, Inc.

Wear-Ever Cookware Set No. 250 $50.00-75.00
Wear-Ever Cookware Set No. 251 $60.00-85.00

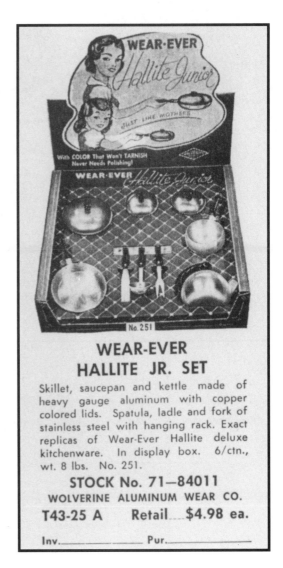

WEAR-EVER HALLITE JR. SET

Skillet, saucepan and kettle made of heavy gauge aluminum with copper colored lids. Spatula, ladle and fork of stainless steel with hanging rack. Exact replicas of Wear-Ever Hallite deluxe kitchenware. In display box. 6/ctn., wt. 8 lbs. No. 251.

STOCK No. 71–84011
WOLVERINE ALUMINUM WEAR CO.

T43-25 A   Retail $4.98 ea.

Inv._____ Pur._____

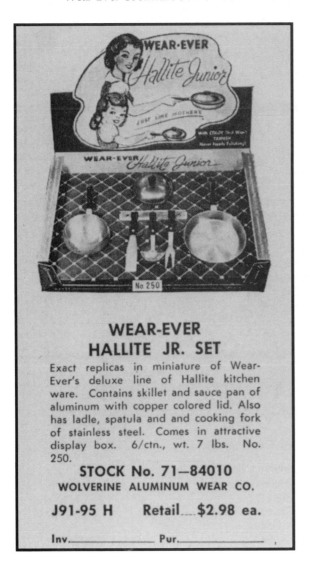

WEAR-EVER HALLITE JR. SET

Exact replicas in miniature of Wear-Ever's deluxe line of Hallite kitchen ware. Contains skillet and sauce pan of aluminum with copper colored lid. Also has ladle, spatula and cooking fork of stainless steel. Comes in attractive display box. 6/ctn., wt. 7 lbs. No. 250.

STOCK No. 71–84010
WOLVERINE ALUMINUM WEAR CO.

J91-95 H   Retail $2.98 ea.

Inv._____ Pur._____

Wear-Ever Cookware Set No. 250

Dover Kitchenware

The toy coffee pot and waffle iron were made by The Dover Manufacturing Company of Dover, Ohio. Both pieces actually worked and were designed to be used by a child who wanted to cook just like mother.

Coffee Pot, 7"	$40.00-45.00
Waffle Iron, 4½"	$55.00-65.00

Aluminum Kitchenware

Bread Pan	$4.00-5.00	Colander	$4.00-5.00
Cake Pan (Plain)	$2.50-3.00	Measure Cup	$4.00-5.00
Cake Pan (Animals)	$3.00-4.00	Mold, spiral	$5.00-8.00
Canister	$8.00-10.00	Muffin Tin	$10.00-12.00
Casserole, covered	$8.00-10.00	Plate	$5.00-8.00
Coffee Pot, 2 pieces	$10.00-12.00	Silverware	$.50-.75
Coffee Pot, 3 pieces	$12.00-16.50	Scoop	$2.00-2.50
Cookie Cutter	$1.00-1.50	Skillet	$4.00-5.00

Mirro Percolator Set

This 2-place child's Percolator Set was marketed by Mirro. The reprint from a 1949 John Plain catalogue, shows another larger Mirro percolator set.

Percolator Set, 2 Places	$40.00-50.00
Percolater Set, 6 Places	$50.00-65.00

Mirro 46-piece Percolator Set

46-Pc. Percolator Set in shiny "MIRRO" aluminum, just like mothers! Contains percolator with glass top and inset, red enameled cover and handle, tray and six each of: cups, saucers, forks, knives, spoons, plates, paper napkins. '3 little Kittens' embossed.
81721 B175 Toy Percolator Set . . **$2.50**

Kiddycook Aluminum Toys

These sets were manufactured by The Aluminum Specialty Company of Manitowoc, Wisconsin during the 1950's.

Coffee Pot Set, 2 Places $35.00-40.00

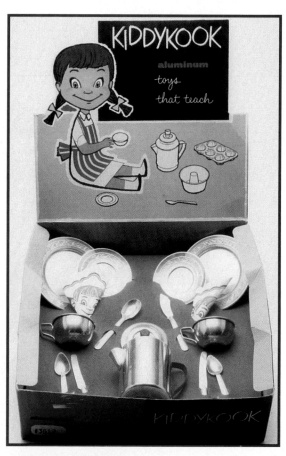

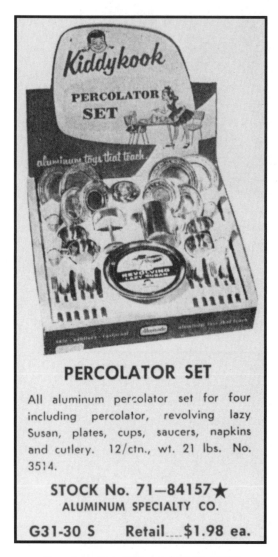

PERCOLATOR SET

All aluminum percolator set for four including percolator, revolving lazy Susan, plates, cups, saucers, napkins and cutlery. 12/ctn., wt. 21 lbs. No. 3514.

STOCK No. 71—84157★
ALUMINUM SPECIALTY CO.

G31-30 S   Retail....$1.98 ea.

Percolator Set, 4 Places $40.00-47.00

PERCOLATOR SET

All aluminum percolator set with complete service for six. Has percolator, lazy Susan, cake cover, plates, cups, saucers, napkins and cutlery plus large plastic table cloth. 6/ctn., wt. 16 lbs. No. 3516.

STOCK No. 71—84158★
ALUMINUM SPECIALTY CO.

G41-95 S   Retail....$2.98 ea.

Percolator Set, 6 Places $50.00-60.00

Aluminum Cook Set

COOK-N-SERVE SET

Safe, durable, practical aluminum pieces. Set has complete service for four with a total of 48 pieces. Has cooking and baking pans and utensils plus dishes and silverware. 6/ctn., wt. 16 lbs. No. 3463.

STOCK No. 71—84064
ALUMINUM SPECIALTY CO.

S81-95 K   Retail____$2.98 ea.

Inv._____ Pur._____

Cook-N-Serv Set $65.00-70.00

Ready Mix Candy Set

CANDY SET

This set contains three boxes of fudge candy ready mix (chocolate—peppermint—butterscotch), large mixing bowl, oblong pan, revolving candy dish and other utensils to make candy. All utensils are aluminum. Comes in attractive display box. 12/ctn., wt. 32 lbs. No. 3575.

STOCK No. 71—84041
ALUMINUM SPECIALTY CO.

G81-30 F   Retail__$1.98 ea.

Inv._____ Pur._____

Candy Set $25.00-35.00

Aluminum Bake Set

ALUMINUM BAKE SET

Cook and bake set made of shiny aluminum consists of muffin pan, mixing bowl, measuring cup, scoop, measuring spoon, fry pan, cake pan, pie pan and two cookie cutters. 12/ctn., wt. 13 lbs. No. 3551.

STOCK No. 71—84020★

ALUMINUM SPECIALTY CO.

G7-65 A   Retail____ $ .98 ea.

Aluminum Bake Set $40.00-45.00

Aluminum Bake Set

ALUMINUM BAKE SET

Large cook and bake set consisting of pressure pan, cake pan, whistling tea kettle, mixing bowl, measuring cup, scoop, fry pan, cookie sheet, muffin pan, and cookie cutters. 12/ctn., wt. 21 lbs. No. 3552.

STOCK No. 71—84027★

ALUMINUM SPECIALTY CO.

Z41-30 R   Retail____ $1.98 ea.

Inv._____ Pur._____

Aluminum Bake Set $45.00-55.00

Ready Mix Cake Set

ANGEL CAKE SET

Kiddy cook angel food cake set includes eight individual angle food cakes. Also includes shiny aluminum cooking utensils such as angel food cake pans, mixing bowl, measuring cup and other items. Real food in packages. 12/ctn., wt. 32 lbs. No. 3577.

STOCK No. 71–84063

ALUMINUM SPECIALTY CO.

G91-95 L   Retail $2.98 ea.

Inv._____   Pur._____

Angel Cake Set $35.00-40.00

Ready Mix Bake Set

READY MIX BAKE SET

This deluxe set combines real food and pure aluminum. Makes 24 tasty treats including angel food cakes, pie fillings, devils food cakes, etc. Has 12 kitchen utensils of shiny aluminum and wood, plus 24 packages of cake mix and frostings. 6/ctn., wt. 25 lbs. No. 3578.

STOCK No. 71–84050

ALUMINUM SPECIALTY CO.

C33-25 D   Retail $4.98 ea.

Inv._____   Pur._____

Ready Mix Bake Set $45.00-55.00

Pressman Baking Set

GINGERBREAD BOY BAKING SET

Story of the gingerbread boy is told inside this book-shaped baking set. Has package of real gingerbread mix, and metal gingerbread boy cookie cutter, measuring cup, spoon, mixing bowl, rolling pin and cookie tray. Receipe book is included. Size 10" x 7" x 2¼". 24/ctn., wt. 25 lbs. No. 1120.

STOCK No. 71—84018 ★

PRESSMAN TOY CORP.

Z6-65 R   Retail____ $ .98 ea.

Inv._____ Pur._____

Pressman Gingerbread Boy Baking Set
$25.00-35.00

Ideal Baking Set

CAKE MIX SET

A 33 piece Betty Crocker junior baking kit including 12 baking mixes and 21 utensils. All food packed in sealed tin foil packages. Colorful instruction book with recipes included. In display box. 12/ctn., wt. 29 lbs. No. 9999.

STOCK No. 71—84066

IDEAL TOY CORP.

G73-25 P   Retail____ $4.98 ea.

Inv._____ Pur._____

Betty Crocker Cake Mix Set
$45.00-50.00

**Little Miss Cookie Cake
Decorating Set**

Boxed Set
$50.00-55.00

Candy Maker Set

Cookie Set

CANDY MAKER SET

Set contains three boxes of quick fudge, cook book, wax paper and metal and wood cooking utensils necessary to make candy. All utensils and ready-to-fix ingredients in attractive package. 12/ctn., wt. 36 lbs. No. K91.

STOCK No. 71—84056★

MODEL CRAFT, INC.

W41-95 E   Retail $2.98 ea.

COOKIE SET

This set features famous Nestle brand cookie mixes and chocolate. Has cookie utensils and accessories that are safe and fool proof.‘ Also includes other cooking ingredients and utensils. In display box. 12/ctn., wt. 36 lbs. No. N31.

STOCK No. 71—84062

MODEL-CRAFT, INC.

R91-95 L   Retail $2.98 ea.

Inv._____   Pur._____

Model Craft Cookie Set
$27.00-35.00

Model Craft Candy Maker Set $25.00-35.00

Wolverine Dutch Scenes

			Canister Set	
Bread Box	$20.00-25.00			
Cake Plate	$5.00-7.50	Coffee		$7.00-8.00
Creamer	$4.00-5.00	Flour		$9.00-10.00
Cup and Saucer	$4.00-5.00	Sugar		$8.00-9.00
Plate	$2.00-3.00	Tea		$6.00-7.00
Sugar	$4.00-5.00	Set, 4 Pieces		$30.00-35.00
Teapot	$18.00-22.00			

Pastry Set

PASTRY SET

Includes workable egg beater, mixing bowl, pastry board and rolling pin, cookie cutters, cannister set and many other kitchen utensils. All items are made of metal and come in decorated box 15 x 20". No. 256.

STOCK No. 71—84034

WOLVERINE SUPPLY & MFG. CO.

B71-30 R   Retail .... $1.98 ea.

Inv._____ Pur._____

Wolverine Pastry Set $50.00-60.00

Tea and Baking Set

TEA AND BAKING SET

Includes complete tea service for four plus cannister set, cookie cutters, rolling pin, pastry board and measuring spoons. Colorful strawberry design. All pieces made of metal. No. 259.

STOCK No. 71—84059

WOLVERINE SUPPLY & MFG. CO.

S21-95 X   Retail .... $2.98 ea.

Inv._____ Pur._____

Wolverine Tea and Baking Set $60.00-80.00

Wolverine Kitchenware

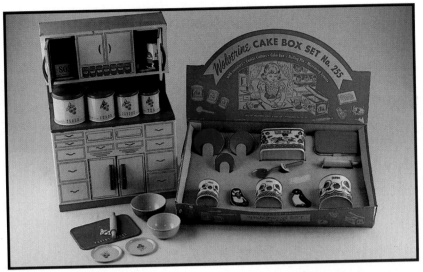

Bake Set, red and yellow, 10 pieces $30.00-35.00
Cabinet $20.00-25.00
Cake Box Set No. 255 $40.00-50.00

Cake Box Set No. 255

CAKE BOX SET

Set contains four canisters; 4 canister lids, plastic measuring spoon, two attractively lithographed cookie cutters, rolling pin, metal cake and bread box. Cover of cake box is used as pastry board. 12 to carton. No. 255.

STOCK No. 71—84019

WOLVERINE SUPPLY & MFG. CO.

X7-65 V   Retail_____ $ .98 ea.

Inv._____ Pur._____

Cake Box Set No. 255 $40.00-50.00

Downyflake Donut Set

DOUGHNUT BAKING SET

Contains three two-ounce bags of genuine doughnut mix, four one-ounce bags of assorted frostings, six compartment aluminum mold, metal egg beater, plastic mixing bowl, spatula and illustration booklet. All in attractive box. 12/ctn., wt. 30 lbs. No. 2220.

STOCK No. 71—84029

PRESSMAN TOY CORP.

A81-30 D   Retail____$1.98 ea.

Inv._____ Pur._____

Pressman Doughnut Baking Set $25.00-30.00

Pastry Sets

Pastry Set in Box $50.00-55.00

PASTRY TABLE and BAKING UTENSILS

Wood and fiber-board table (16x12 1/2 in. top) just the right height for a little pastry cook (17 inches). With plastic meat grinder, metal egg beater, 2 plastic mixing bowls, pastry board, rolling pin, cake turner, 2 bread pans, 2 fluted pans, potato masher, 3 cookie cutters, assorted spoons, recipes.

81219 B210 Retail Price $2.98

Pastry Table, and Baking Utensils

Little Busy Baker
Pastry Set No. 5902

$60.00-70.00
$30.00-35.00

Little Homemaker Cooking Set

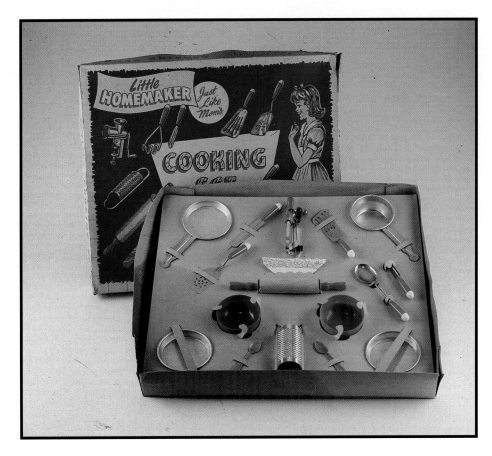

Boxed Set $50.00-55.00

Wolverine Corner Grocer

Corner Grocer Set $140.00-150.00

Kitchen Utensils

Utensil Set $50.00-60.00

Cake Mix Set (Model Craft)

CAKE MIX SET

A 40-pc. set which contains everything to bake except milk. Has three kinds of Pillsbury cake mix; chocolate fudge, golden yellow, snowy white. Enough to bake nine cakes, frostings and decorations. All utensils needed. Easy to understand cook book. 12 to carton. No. P71.

STOCK No. 71—84060 ★
MODEL-CRAFT, INC.

W21-95 E   Retail_____$2.98 ea.

Inv._____   Pur._____

Cake Mix Set $35.00-40.00

Heinz Kitchen (Model Craft)

HEINZ KITCHEN

Heinz Kitchen is a realistic, attractive plaything containing one cabinet, six cans of Heinz foods, two bowls, two plates, and many other items including casserole dish, sauce pan, chef's hat and cook book. Walls of cabinet may be decorated. No. H57.

STOCK No. 71—84055 ★
MODEL CRAFT, INC.

H43-25 A   Retail___$4.98 ea.

Inv._____   Pur._____

Kitchen Set $60.00-65.00

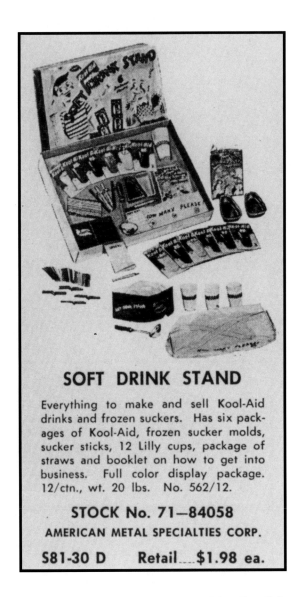

**Soft Drink Stand
(American Metal Specialties Corp.)**

Soft Drink Set $35.00-45.00

SOFT DRINK STAND

Everything to make and sell Kool-Aid drinks and frozen suckers. Has six packages of Kool-Aid, frozen sucker molds, sucker sticks, 12 Lilly cups, package of straws and booklet on how to get into business. Full color display package. 12/ctn., wt. 20 lbs. No. 562/12.

STOCK No. 71—84058
AMERICAN METAL SPECIALTIES CORP.

S81-30 D   Retail___$1.98 ea.

Play Food Set (Ohio Art)

Play Food Set $45.00-50.00

Chuck Wagon Set
(American Metal Specialties Corp.)

CHUCK WAGON SET

Famous Campbell kid's chuck wagon set contains cans of spaghetti, pork and beans, soup plus kettle, plates, mugs, silverware, ladle and Campbell Kid's Chuck Wagon Cookbook. Also has Western neckerchief and phonograph record with Western tune. 6/ctn., wt. 35½ lbs. No. 516/6.

STOCK No. 71—84070★
AMERICAN METAL SPECIALTIES CO.

D73-25 L   Retail $4.98 ea.

Inv._____ Pur._____

Chuck Wagon Set
$55.00-60.00

Campbell Kids Set
(American Metal Specialties Corp.)

CAMPBELL KIDS SET

A cooking set including six filled cans of Campbell Soup. Pantry shelf type box includes many cooking utensils such as soup ladle, soup bowls, sauce pan, measuring cup, etc. Also includes Campbell's Kids Chef's apron and hat. 6/ctn., wt. 5 lbs. No. 512/6.

STOCK No. 71—84069
AMERICAN METAL SPECIALTIES

G43-25 P   Retail $4.98 ea.

Inv._____ Pur._____

Campbell Kids Set
$50.00-60.00

Ohio Art Tea Sets

Little Red Riding Hood
  2-place Set $45.00-55.00
Cinderella 2-place Set $40.00-50.00
Mother Goose
  2-place Set $45.00-55.00

Fruits Tea Set (Ohio Art)

15 PIECE TEA SET

This all metal set will stand up for years. All edges turned for safety; brightly lithographed. Include 5" x 7" tray, 4 cups, 4 saucers, 4 plates, tea pot and lid. 24 per carton, wt. 15 lbs. No. 65.

STOCK No. 71—84135

OHIO ART CO.

H4-46 M   Retail .... $ .69 ea.

Tea Set in Box
$25.00-35.00

Blue Willow Child's Set
(Ohio Art)

21-PIECE TEA SET

Set is attractively packaged in two color display box and a pieces are securely attached to heavy printed filler. Decorate n four color litho. Set contains 21 pieces. 12 to carto wt. 18 lbs. No. 172.

STOCK No. 71—84145

OHIO ART CO.

K3-65 M   Retail .... $ .98 ea

nv. _____ Pur. _____

Blue Willow Set
$65.00-85.00

Ohio Art Tea Sets

Fairies, 4-Place Set	$35.00-45.00
Pinocchio, 4-Place Set	$75.00-85.00

Ohio Art Tea Sets

Children, 4-Place Set	$35.00-45.00
Rabbits and Balloons, 4-Place Set	$35.00-45.00

Ohio Art Tea Sets

Little Red Riding Hood 14-Piece Boxed Set $50.00-55.00
Floral 18-Piece Boxed Set $35.00-45.00

J. Chein and Company Tea Sets

Strawberry 4-Place Set $25.00-35.00
Candy Cane 4-Place Set $25.00-35.00

American Modern by Russell Wright (Ideal)

This child's plastic set was advertised in a 1950's Ideal catalogue. There were three sizes of sets available. Prices ranged from 98 cents to $2.98.

Boxed Set, 3 places $100.00-125.00

American Modern Dinnerware

Casserole	$25.00-35.00
Gravy Boat	$20.00-25.00
Platter	$15.00-18.00

American Airlines Stewardess Set

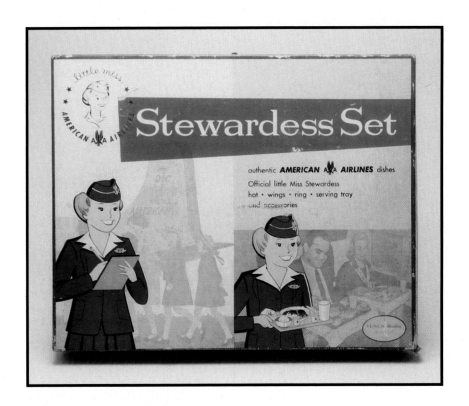

The American Airlines Stewardess Set was produced by the Toy Division of Venus Pen and Pencil Corporation of Hoboken, New Jersey. The set included "Miss Stewardess" wings, hat and ring, play dishes, napkins, menu, seat assignment chart, and flight training certificate.

Stewardess Set $60.00-65.00

Plastic Tea Set (Irwin Corp.)

Tea Set, 2 Places $20.00-25.00

Plastic Tea Set (Irwin Corp.)

Plastic Tea Set (Irwin Corp.)

TEA SET

Ebony and gold tea set with service for four. A 28-piece set consisting of tea pot with spigot, sugar bowl, creamer, cups, plates, saucers and cutlery. Each piece is ebony decorated in gold. 6/ctn., wt. 27 lbs. No. 9111.

STOCK No. 71—84152

IRWIN CORP.

R72-60 A   Retail....$3.98 ea.

Inv._____ Pur._____

TEA SET

Third dimensional antique gold service for six. A 43-piece set including tea pot with spigot, sugar bowl, creamer, salt and pepper shaker, and other items. Every item has attractive design with new 3-D rims in antique gold. 6/ctn., wt. 44 lbs. No. 9127.

STOCK No. 71—84153

IRWIN CORP.

L83-90 R   Retail....$5.98 ea.

Tea Set, 4 Places $30.00-35.00

Tea Set, 6 Places $35.00-45.00

Children's Dishes

Plastic Blue Willow Tea Set (Ideal)

This plastic Blue Willow tea set was produced by the Ideal Toy and Novelty Company of Hollis, New York. The four-place setting includes a teapot, sugar, creamer, cups, saucers, silverware and napkins.

Boxed Set, 4 places
$65.00-75.00

Plastic Tea Set (Irwin Corp.)

Plastic Tea Set (Irwin Corp.)

TEA SET

Gay Victorian tea set wtih complete service for four. A 28-piece set consisting of tea pot with spigot, creamer, sugar bowl, cups, plates, saucers, and cutlery. All items have floral design, cutlery is white. 6/ctn., wt. 27 lbs. No. 9071.

STOCK No. 71—84151
IRWIN CORP.

Z31-95 R   Retail .... $2.98 ea.

Inv. _____ Pur. _____

Boxed Tea Set $30.00-35.00

TEA SET

Miss Butterfinger's polyethylene tea set contains 40-pieces, service for six. Includes tea pot with spigot, sugar bowl, creamer, cups, plates, saucers and cutlery. All items have attractive design and are unbreakable. 6/ctn., wt. 33 lbs. No. 9134.

STOCK No. 71—84141★
IRWIN CORP.

G32-60 R   Retail ... $3.98 ea.

Inv. _____ Pur. _____

Boxed Tea Set $35.00-40.00

Plastic Tea Sets (Irwin Corp.)

TEA SET

Miss Butterfinger's polyethylene tea set with complete service for two, 16 pieces. Has tea pot with spigot, sugar bowl, creamer, cups, plates, saucers and cutlery. All items are attractively decorated in green and white. 12/ctn., wt. 10 lbs. No. 9137.

STOCK No. 71—84126

IRWIN CORP.

T31-30 A   Retail___$1.98 ea.

Inv._____   Pur._____

Boxed Tea Set $25.00-30.00

TEA SET

A 12-piece tea set containing service for two. Consists of cups, saucers, knives, forks, spoons, creamer and sugar bowl. All items are in attractive colors in Florentine design. 12/ctn., wt. 12 lbs. No. 9040.

STOCK No. 71—84090

IRWIN CORP.

H4-65 L   Retail___$ .98 ea.

Inv._____   Pur._____

Boxed Tea Set $20.00-25.00

TEA SET

Miss Butterfinger's polyethylene tea set with service for 4. A 28 piece set consisting of tea pot with spigot, sugar bowl, creamer, cups, plates, saucers and cutlery. Cups and cutlery in sky blue, rest in white and blue. 6/ctn., wt. 25 lbs. No. 9133.

STOCK No. 71—84130

IRWIN CORP.

T31-95 A   Retail___$2.98 ea.

Inv._____   Pur._____

Boxed Tea Set $30.00-35.00

FLORENTINE TEA SET

Service for two, 16 pieces consisting of tea pot with spigot, sugar bowl, creamer, cups, plates, saucers and cutlery. All pieces have beautiful design and cutlery is in Silva-glo. In lithographed window display box. 12/ctn., wt. 12 lbs. No. 9108.

STOCK No. 71—84125

IRWIN CORP.

G41-30 A   Retail___$1.98 ea.

Inv._____   Pur._____

Boxed Tea Set $20.00-25.00

Plastic Sets

Banner Chocolate Set	$30.00-35.00
"Alice" Tea Set	$30.00-35.00
Plastic Silverware Set	$18.00-22.00

Plastic Tea Set (Banner)

GOLDEN GLO TEA SET

This is a 40 piece set with service for six. Consists of plates, saucers, cups, cutlery, tea pot, cover, creamer and sugar bowl. Colorful design on all items. Table ware in metal-tone "gold-like" finish. Each in display box. 6/ctn. No. 1820.

STOCK No. 71—84131■★

BANNER PLASTICS CORP.

D71-95 R   Retail___$2.98 ea.

Inv._____   Pur._____

Boxed Tea Set $25.00-35.00

Plastic Tea Set (Banner)

TEA SET

June rose tea set contains 29 pieces, service for four. Dishes are white with rose design and blue rims. Table ware is in Metaltone "silver-like" finish. In decorated display box. 12/ctn. No. 1216.

STOCK No. 71—84127■★

BANNER PLASTICS CORP.

J91-30 N   Retail___$1.98 ea.

Inv._____   Pur._____

Boxed Tea Set $25.00-35.00

Alice in Wonderland Tea Set

This is a celluloid tea set with only the sugar, creamer, and teapot bearing the "Alice" portrait.
Set, 4 Places $70.00-80.00

Plastic Kitchenware Set (Banner)

Plastic Tableware (Banner)

TEA STAND WITH COPPER KETTLE

A 10-piece set consisting of four each plastic cups and saucers; all metal stand on which cups can be hung and plates mounted, plastic tea kettle in metal tone copper like finish. Each in colorful display box. No. 1210.

STOCK No. 71—84132★

BANNER PLASTICS CORP.

G61-62 T   Retail $2.49 ea.

Inv._____ Pur._____

Kitchenware Set $40.00-45.00

METAL TONE TABLEWARE

An 18 piece set finished in Banner's metaltone (silver-like) finish. Packaged in unusual wood grain hinged box with window fronts. Box size 15" x 10" x 1¼". Comes 24 to carton. No. 680.

STOCK No. 71—84211

BANNER PLASTICS CORP.

W6-65 X   Retail $ .98 ea.

Inv._____ Pur._____

Set in Box $15.00-20.00

Plastic Tea Set (Worcester)

Tea Set in Box $20.00-30.00

Plastic Tea Set (Worcester)

TEA SET

Polyethylene fiesta tea set with attractive design. This soft plastic set is unbreakable and has service for four, including cups, saucers and spoons. Comes in attractive colors. 24/ctn., No. 281.

STOCK No. 71—84088
WORCESTER TOY CO.

K6-65 R   Retail $ .98 ea.

Inv._____   Pur._____

Boxed Set $20.00-30.00

Plastic Tea Set (Worcester)

PAINT YOUR OWN TEA SET

Big top paint your own tea set contains 14 pieces including cups, saucers, 6'' plates, tea pot, creamer, sugar bowl, and paint brush with paint containers. All items are white and four colors of paint are included. 12/ctn. No. 270.

STOCK No. 71—84089
WORCESTER TOY CO.

Y31-30 W   Retail $1.98 ea.

Inv._____   Pur._____

Boxed Set $20.00-25.00

Bibliography

Florence, Gene. *The Collector's Encyclopedia of Akro Agate Glassware.*
Collector Books, Paducah, Kentucky, 1975.

Florence, Gene. *The Collector's Encyclopedia of Depression Glass.*
Collector Books, Paducah, Kentucky, 1992.

Florence, Gene. *Collectible Glassware from the 40's, 50's & 60's.*
Collector Books, Paducah, Kentucky, 1992.

Hartung, Marion T. and Hinshaw, Iona E. *Patterns and Pinfores-Pressed Toy Dishes
Book II.* Wallace Homestead Company. Des Moines, Iowa, 1978.

Heacock, William. *Encyclopedia of Victorian Colored Pattern Glass.*
Antique Publications, Marietta, Ohio, 1976.

Kamm, Minnie W. and Serry Wood, ed. *Encyclopedia of Antique Pattern Glass.*
Century House, Watkins Glen, New York, 1961.

Lechler, Doris, *English Toy China*, 1989, Antique Publications, Marietta, Ohio.

Lechler, Doris. *Toy Glass.* Antique Publications, Marietta, Ohio, 1989.

Lechler, Doris and Virginia O' Neill. *Children's Glass Dishes.*
Thomas Nelson, Inc. Publishers, Nashville, Tennesee, 1976.

Lee, Ruth Webb. *Ruth Webb Lee's Handbook of Early American Pressed Glass
Patterns.* Lee Publications, Wellesly Hills, Massachusetts, 1964.

Metz, Alice Hulet. *Early American Pattern Glass.* Spencer Walker Press,
Columbus, Ohio, 1971.

Mlller, Robert W. ed. *Price Guide to Antiques and Pattern Glass, 6th ed.* Wallace
Homestead Book Company, Des Moines, Iowa, 1979.

Sandwich Historical Society. *The Sandwich Glass Museum Collection.*
The Sandwich Glass Museum, Sandwich Massachusetts, 1969.

Books on Antiques and Collectibles

Most of the following books are available from your local book seller or antique dealer, or on loan from your public library. If you are unable to locate certain titles in your area you may order by mail from COLLECTOR BOOKS, P.O. Box 3009, Paducah, KY 42002-3009. This is only a partial listing of the books on antiques that are available from Collector Books. All books are well illustrated and contain current values. Add $2.00 for postage for the first book ordered and $.30 for each additional book. Include item number, title and price when ordering. Allow 14 to 21 days for delivery.

BOOKS ON GLASS AND POTTERY

1810	American Art Glass, Shuman	$29.95
2016	Bedroom & Bathroom Glassware of the Depression Years	$19.95
1312	Blue & White Stoneware, McNerney	$9.95
1959	Blue Willow, 2nd Ed., Gaston	$14.95
2270	Collectible Glassware from the 40's, 50's, & 60's, Florence	$19.95
3311	Collecting Yellow Ware - Id. & Value Gd., McAllister	$16.95
2352	Collector's Ency. of Akro Agate Glassware, Florence	$14.95
1373	Collector's Ency. of American Dinnerware, Cunningham	$24.95
2272	Collector's Ency. of California Pottery, Chipman	$24.95
3312	Collector's Ency. of Children's Dishes, Whitmyer	$19.95
2133	Collector's Ency. of Cookie Jars, Roerig	$24.95
2273	Collector's Ency. of Depression Glass, 10th Ed., Florence	$19.95
2209	Collector's Ency. of Fiesta, 7th Ed., Huxford	$19.95
1439	Collector's Ency. of Flow Blue China, Gaston	$19.95
1915	Collector's Ency. of Hall China, 2nd Ed., Whitmyer	$19.95
2334	Collector's Ency. of Majolica Pottery, Katz-Marks	$19.95
1358	Collector's Ency. of McCoy Pottery, Huxford	$19.95
3313	Collector's Ency. of Niloak, Gifford	$19.95
1039	Collector's Ency. of Nippon Porcelain I, Van Patten	$19.95
2089	Collector's Ency. of Nippon Porcelain II, Van Patten	$24.95
1665	Collector's Ency. of Nippon Porcelain III, Van Patten	$24.95
1034	Collector's Ency. of Roseville Pottery, Huxford	$19.95
1035	Collector's Ency. of Roseville Pottery, 2nd Ed., Huxford	$19.95
3314	Collector's Ency. of Van Briggle Art Pottery, Sasicki	$24.95
2339	Collector's Guide to Shawnee Pottery, Vanderbilt	$19.95
1425	Cookie Jars, Westfall	$9.95
2275	Czechoslovakian Glass & Collectibles, Barta	$16.95
3315	Elegant Glassware of the Depression Era, 5th Ed., Florence	$19.95
3318	Glass Animals of the Depression Era, Garmon & Spencer	$19.95
2024	Kitchen Glassware of the Depression Years, 4th Ed., Florence	$19.95
2379	Lehner's Ency. of U.S. Marks on Pottery, Porcelain & Clay	$24.95
2394	Oil Lamps II, Thuro	$24.95
3322	Pocket Guide to Depression Glass, 8th Ed., Florence	$9.95
2345	Portland Glass, Ladd	$24.95
1670	Red Wing Collectibles, DePasquale	$9.95
1440	Red Wing Stoneware, DePasquale	$9.95
1958	So. Potteries Blue Ridge Dinnerware, 3rd Ed., Newbound	$14.95
2221	Standard Carnival Glass, 3rd Ed., Edwards	$24.95
1848	Very Rare Glassware of the Depression Years, Florence	$24.95
2140	Very Rare Glassware of the Depression Years, Second Series	$24.95
3326	Very Rare Glassware of the Depression Era, Third Series	$24.95
3327	Watt Pottery - Identification & Value Guide, Morris	$19.95
2224	World of Salt Shakers, 2nd Ed., Lechner	$24.95

BOOKS ON DOLLS & TOYS

2079	Barbie Fashion, Vol. 1, 1959-1967, Eames	$24.95
3310	Black Dolls - 1820-1990 - Id. & Value Guide, Perkins	$17.95
1514	Character Toys & Collectibles 1st Series, Longest	$19.95
1750	Character Toys & Collectibles, 2nd Series, Longest	$19.95
1529	Collector's Ency. of Barbie Dolls, DeWein	$19.95
2338	Collector's Ency. of Disneyana, Longest & Stern	$24.95
2342	Madame Alexander Price Guide #17, Smith	$9.95
1540	Modern Toys, 1930-1980, Baker	$19.95
2343	Patricia Smith's Doll Values Antique to Modern, 8th ed	$12.95
1886	Stern's Guide to Disney	$14.95

2139	Stern's Guide to Disney, 2nd Series	$14.95
1513	Teddy Bears & Steiff Animals, Mandel	$9.95
1817	Teddy Bears & Steiff Animals, 2nd, Mandel	$19.95
2084	Teddy Bears, Annalees & Steiff Animals, 3rd, Mandel	$19.95
2028	Toys, Antique & Collectible, Longest	$14.95
1808	Wonder of Barbie, Manos	$9.95
1430	World of Barbie Dolls, Manos	$9.95

OTHER COLLECTIBLES

1457	American Oak Furniture, McNerney	$9.95
2269	Antique Brass & Copper, Gaston	$16.95
2333	Antique & Collectible Marbles, 3rd Ed., Grist,	$9.95
1712	Antique & Collectible Thimbles, Mathis	$19.95
1748	Antique Purses, Holiner	$19.95
1868	Antique Tools, Our American Heritage, McNerney	$9.95
1426	Arrowheads & Projectile Points, Hothem	$7.95
1278	Art Nouveau & Art Deco Jewelry, Baker	$9.95
1714	Black Collectibles, Gibbs	$19.95
1128	Bottle Pricing Guide, 3rd Ed., Cleveland	$7.95
1751	Christmas Collectibles, Whitmyer	$19.95
1752	Christmas Ornaments, Johnston	$19.95
2132	Collector's Ency. of American Furniture, Vol. I, Swedberg	$24.95
2271	Collector's Ency. of American Furniture, Vol. II, Swedberg	$24.95
2338	Collector's Ency. of Disneyana, Longest & Stern	$24.95
2018	Collector's Ency. of Graniteware, Greguire	$24.95
2083	Collector's Ency. of Russel Wright Designs, Kerr	$19.95
2337	Collector's Guide to Decoys, Book II, Huxford	$16.95
2340	Collector's Guide to Easter Collectibles, Burnett	$16.95
1441	Collector's Guide to Post Cards, Wood	$9.95
2276	Decoys, Kangas	$24.95
1629	Doorstops, Id. & Values, Bertoia	$9.95
1716	Fifty Years of Fashion Jewelry, Baker	$19.95
3316	Flea Market Trader, 8th Ed., Huxford	$9.95
3317	Florence's Standard Baseball Card Price Gd., 5th Ed.	$9.95
1755	Furniture of the Depression Era, Swedberg	$19.95
2278	Grist's Machine Made & Contemporary Marbles	$9.95
1424	Hatpins & Hatpin Holders, Baker	$9.95
3319	Huxford's Collectible Advertising - Id. & Value Gd.	$17.95
1181	100 Years of Collectible Jewelry, Baker	$9.95
2023	Keen Kutter Collectibles, 2nd Ed., Heuring	$14.95
2216	Kitchen Antiques - 1790-1940, McNerney	$14.95
3320	Modern Guns - Id. & Val. Gd., 9th Ed., Quertermous	$12.95
1965	Pine Furniture, Our Am. Heritage, McNerney	$14.95
3321	Ornamental & Figural Nutcrackers, Rittenhouse	$16.95
2026	Railroad Collectibles, 4th Ed., Baker	$14.95
1632	Salt & Pepper Shakers, Guarnaccia	$9.95
1888	Salt & Pepper Shakers II, Guarnaccia	$14.95
2220	Salt & Pepper Shakers III, Guarnaccia	$14.95
3323	Schroeder's Antique Price Guide, 11th Ed.	$12.95
3324	Schroeder's Antique & Coll. 1993 Engag. Calendar	$9.95
2346	Sheet Music Ref. & Price Guide, Pafik & Guiheen	$18.95
2096	Silverplated Flatware, 4th Ed., Hagan	$14.95
3325	Standard Knife Collector's Guide, Stewart	$12.95
2348	20th Century Fashionable Plastic Jewelry, Baker	$19.95
2349	Value Guide to Baseball Collectibles, Raycraft	$16.95

Schroeder's
ANTIQUES
Price Guide

... is the #1 best-selling antiques & collectibles value guide on the market today, and here's why . . .

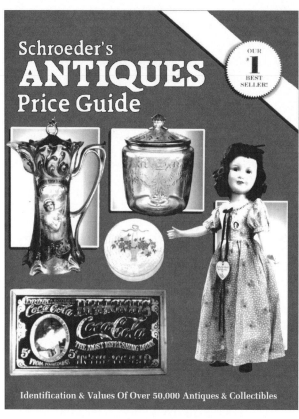

**Schroeder's
ANTIQUES
Price Guide**

OUR #1 BEST SELLER!

Identification & Values Of Over 50,000 Antiques & Collectibles

8½ x 11, 608 Pages, $12.95

• More than 300 advisors, well-known dealers, and top-notch collectors work together with our editors to bring you accurate information regarding pricing and identification.

• More than 45,000 items in almost 500 categories are listed along with hundreds of sharp original photos that illustrate not only the rare and unusual, but the common, popular collectibles as well.

• Each large close-up shot shows important details clearly. Every subject is represented with histories and background information, a feature not found in any of our competitors' publications.

• Our editors keep abreast of newly developing trends, often adding several new categories a year as the need arises.

If it merits the interest of today's collector, you'll find it in *Schroeder's*. And you can feel confident that the information we publish is up to date and accurate. Our advisors thoroughly check each category to spot inconsistencies, listings that may not be entirely reflective of market dealings, and lines too vague to be of merit. Only the best of the lot remains for publication.

Without doubt, you'll find
SCHROEDER'S ANTIQUES PRICE GUIDE
the only one to buy for
reliable information and values.

COLLECTOR BOOKS
A Division of Schroeder Publishing Co., Inc.